DON'T TAKE YOUR SHOES OFF YET

JONATHAN ALLEN, JR.

VISION PUBLISHING
HOUSE

Vision Publishing House
support@vision-publishinghouse.com
www.vision-publishinghouse.com

ISBN: 979-8-9933667-3-9 (print)
LCCN: 2025922119

This book is established to provide information and inspiration to all readers. It is designed with the understanding that the author is not engaged to render any psychological, legal, or any other kind of professional advice. The content is the sole expression of the author. The author is not liable for any physical, psychological, emotional, financial, or commercial damages, including, but not limited to special, incidental, consequential, or other damages. All readers are responsible for their own choices, actions, and results.

To those who have lost their way...

"Just doing MY heart."

JONATHAN ALLEN, JR.

CONTENTS

INTRODUCTION

You didn't stumble upon this book by accident. Perhaps a whisper, a stirring, or even a silent frustration—led you here. Maybe it's the feeling that you've done a lot, but you're still not done. Maybe you've climbed mountains others only dream about, but something deep inside still says, "There's more."

This book is for those standing at the intersection of accomplishment and assignment—those who've celebrated victories but feel God tugging them forward. It's for those who sense that purpose doesn't end at the finish line, because in the Kingdom, every finish is actually a new beginning.

You might be tired. You might feel like you've earned the right to sit down, take off your shoes, and finally rest. But deep down, you know the mission isn't complete. Your story isn't over. Your impact isn't finished. And the people assigned to your voice, your gift, and your obedience are still waiting.

This isn't just another motivational message wrapped in clichés. This is a soul-check. A recalibration. A wake-up call to anyone who has ever felt the temptation to settle just short of destiny. It's a challenge to stay laced up, even when the path is unfamiliar, uncomfortable, or unclear.

There's a reason you couldn't ignore the nudge to pick this up. And it's because God isn't finished with you.

So if you're ready to lean into the next layer of your purpose—not just for applause, but for impact...

If you're willing to examine what you've carried, what you've created, and what you've yet to release...

If you're courageous enough to admit that your "pause" might have turned into "park"—this book is your sign to move again.

Keep your shoes on. There's still room to do more.

CHAPTER 1
WHO THE HELL ARE YOU?

W *ho?* At first glance, it's a simple question—one you might think you can answer without hesitation. But when you strip away the surface-level answers—the roles you play, the titles you hold, and the things you do—it becomes much harder to define. The truth is, many of us live our lives never truly understanding who we are at our core. Instead, we let others define us, or worse, we define ourselves based on external circumstances.

To begin this journey of self-discovery, you must first understand where you come from. Your identity doesn't begin and end with you. Who you are today is shaped, in part, by those who came before you—your parents, grandparents, and even generations further back. Traits like fear, anger, complacency, or even drive and ambition often run deeper than we realize. We carry patterns, habits, and behaviors passed down through family dynamics, sometimes unknowingly.

Perhaps you've inherited your mother's communication struggles, your father's work ethic, or your grandmother's resilience. Or maybe you carry traits from generations you've never met—traits that skipped your parents and landed in you. Until you recognize these influences, both good and bad, you can't fully understand yourself or where you're headed.

Identity is the foundation for everything else in life. If you don't know who you are, you'll wander aimlessly, easily swayed by opinions, circumstances, or societal pressures. You'll find yourself lost, drifting without purpose or direction. But when you begin to uncover your true identity—when you dig deep into who you really are—you create a solid foundation to build on.

This is the journey we'll embark on in this book: peeling back the layers, confronting truths about yourself, and discovering the power of knowing who you are. It won't be easy, and it won't always be comfortable, but it will be worth it. Because once you know where you come from, you'll finally see where you're going. So, I ask you now: *Who the hell are you?*

Let's find out together.

THE ROUND TABLE SESSION

Every journey begins with a moment—a spark that changes everything. For me, it happened during a time when I thought I was just working on a project. I didn't know it then, but what began as a simple day of searching for a workspace would set me on the path to discovering who I truly was.

In 2010, I found myself in Duluth Georgia, working on what felt like a promising creative venture with two business partners. At the time, we were chasing something bigger than ourselves: we wanted to build a web series that showcased collaboration, creativity, and what two Black-owned brands could achieve together. This was at the very beginning of the vlogging era—when video blogging was just starting to pick up steam—and we knew we had a unique idea that could make waves.

The project was ambitious. We weren't just creating content; we were building something that could inspire others to see possibility, partnership, and innovation in ways they hadn't before. The energy between the three of us was undeniable, but the journey was anything but easy. We were bootstrapping the entire process, relying on whatever resources we could scrape together to make it happen. Every decision, every meeting, and every small victory felt critical to our success.

One day, we planned to work out of an office space. My friend Millie, who was connected to his college's media center, had offered it to us temporarily, and we were looking forward to finally having a place to focus and strategize. But when we arrived, the doors were locked. The space was unavailable, and just like that, our plans for the day were derailed.

Everyone else seemed to accept the setback. My partners were ready to leave, calling it a wasted trip. I, on the other hand, couldn't let it go. As we stood outside the building, I noticed a sign—almost as if it was waiting for me. It read: "Furniture on Sale Upstairs."

Now, to anyone else, it was just a sign. But to me, it felt like a breadcrumb. All we needed to get our work done was a simple desk— some kind of conference room setup where we could brainstorm, plan, and create. I figured, Why not check it out?

"I'm going upstairs," I said, heading back toward the building.

"Where are you going?" one of my partners asked, shooting me a look like I was crazy.

"To see what's up there," I replied.

"Man, don't go up there. There's nothing for us upstairs," they warned.

Their doubt didn't matter to me. Something in me was curious, and curiosity has always been a driving force in my life. When other people turn back, I tend to push forward. I thought, Maybe there's something up there for us. Maybe there's not. But we won't know unless we look.

And so, while they hesitated, I kept walking. Of course, eventually, they followed—partly out of curiosity and partly because, let's be honest, no one wants to be the one left behind.

When we reached the top floor, I saw that the door was cracked open, just slightly. It was one of those moments where you could feel something on the other side—an opportunity, an unknown. I pushed the door open a little wider and called out, "Hello?"

From somewhere in the back of the room, a voice responded, "Hello! We're in the back."

The six of us stepped into the room, unsure of what we were walking into. It was a big space—simple, but it felt intentional. At the center of the room was a round table, huge windows with the sun shining in and seated were three or four people, all facing a woman who was standing at the front of the room speaking.

It was clear that we had interrupted something—a class or a meeting, maybe. But instead of feeling out of place, I felt drawn to that table. The woman proceeded to ask us to have a seat and without thinking twice, I walked straight to it and sat down at the head of the table.

At that moment, it was instinct. I didn't consider what anyone else thought, where they were sitting, or whether I belonged there. The head of the table called to me, and I answered.

I could feel the eyes of the people in the room shift toward me, and then I heard her voice:

"Why did you sit there?"

The room was quiet.

The question caught me off guard, but I didn't hesitate. It wasn't an accusatory question, but it carried weight. It felt as though she was asking something much deeper than what it seemed on the surface. The silence that followed was the kind that makes you hyper-aware of everything—every eye on you, every breath, every thought racing through your mind.

Without skipping a beat, I replied, "I always sit at the head of the table."

There was no arrogance in my answer—it was just my truth. For as long as I could remember, I'd noticed the unspoken significance of the head of the table. Whether it was family dinners on Sunday nights, holiday gatherings, or formal meetings, the person at the head wasn't just a participant—they were the participant. The leader. The one with responsibility. The one who carried weight.

As a kid, I would watch my father, or maybe my uncle or grandfather, take that seat. They didn't always announce it, but there was an air about them—a quiet authority that came with being at the head. I never asked questions about it, but I noticed. I picked it up, little by little, internalizing it without even realizing it.

Years later, I found myself instinctively drawn to the same seat. Maybe it was a habit. Maybe it was comfort. Or maybe, deep down, it was something more.

The woman didn't let up. She studied me for a moment, her expression unreadable. She looked at me as if I had answered correctly, but still missed something. There was curiosity in her eyes, but also a hint of recognition—like she saw something in me that I couldn't yet see in myself.

She tilted her head slightly, studying me.

"What's your name?" she asked, breaking the silence.

"Jonathan," I said, my voice steady.

The way she nodded told me she wasn't just asking for information —she was probing, peeling back layers I didn't even know I had.

Her eyes didn't leave mine. "Do you know who Jonathan was in the Bible?" she asked next.

I didn't hesitate. "Yes," I said confidently. "He was David's best friend. He was loyal."

Her face softened just slightly, almost like she was both surprised and impressed. "Oh, okay. You know something," she said.

It felt like a small exchange, but something about the way she said it stuck with me. I could tell she was evaluating me—not in a judgmental way, but in a way that made me feel seen. I felt she saw something deeper in me.

The room settled, and the conversation resumed. The woman turned her attention back to the group, continuing her teaching, as if nothing unusual had happened. But for me, everything had shifted.

As I sat there, her words and my own answers replayed in my head.

Why did I sit at the head of the table? Why did that seat feel so natural, so right?

Was it just because I had watched others take that seat growing up? Was it just a habit, or was there something more to it? Maybe it wasn't just about confidence or leadership. Maybe it was about stepping into a space that I was destined for—a place I didn't fully understand yet, but one I was drawn to nonetheless.

For the first time, I started to think about what it meant. Isn't that how life works sometimes? We instinctively make choices that reflect parts of our identity, even before we fully recognize who we are. I didn't sit there because I thought I was better than anyone else. I sat there because that place was mine, and felt natural– even familiar. But in truth, I didn't know the deeper *why*.

As the lesson continued, the woman's attention seemed to keep circling back to me. It was as if the energy in the room shifted. Then, she asked another question—not to the group, but directly to me:

"When you and your partners go out to conduct business, who speaks?"

It was such a simple question, but it hit harder than it should have. Why? Because just before we arrived at the building—literally 45 minutes earlier—my business partners had been drilling me in the car about this exact issue.

"You need to speak more," they told me.

"People listen when you talk. Things move when you open your mouth."

But I brushed it off. I was tired of always being the one to speak because many were afraid to do their part. Growing up, I was *that* kid. I was the one everyone turned to for answers when no one else knew what to say. Whether it was in church or in class, people always looked at me. I was the one expected to step up, and honestly, I was over it.

So, I answered her honestly: "I don't speak because I've been doing it my whole life."

She nodded, listening. Then, she paused for a moment and asked me something that stopped me in my tracks: "Who are you?"

With no hesitation and not one thought, I went straight into what I knew: "I'm a business owner. I'm a drummer. I'm a traveler."

She shook her head, interrupting me. "No. I didn't ask you what *you do*. I asked: *Who are you?*"

And just like that, I froze. Her words cut deeper than I expected. I sat there, unable to respond. For the first time in my life, I realized I didn't know the answer to that question. I knew the roles I played, the things I was good at, and the activities that filled my time. But that wasn't who I was. It was just the surface.

I was stuck.

No one had ever asked me that before—not like this. And I didn't have an answer.

That moment—sitting at the head of the table, being confronted with the question "Who are you?"— was the spark that started it all. It forced me to reflect on something I had never really considered before. I thought I knew myself, but I didn't. I had nothing to say beyond a list of accomplishments and hobbies. It forced me to look deeper—to start asking myself questions I'd been avoiding:

- Who am I beyond what I do?
- What do I stand for?
- What values define me?

It was uncomfortable, but it was necessary. And I think that's true for most of us. We're so used to defining ourselves by our jobs, talents, or roles that we forget those are just pieces of the puzzle. They're not *who we are.*

That day, I didn't have the answers. But it sparked something in me—a need to figure it out. I had to confront the parts of myself I'd ignored. I had to start digging deep to discover my true identity. That woman's challenge stayed with me: stop defining yourself by what you do and start discovering who you are.

It's a question I pass on to you now, not to intimidate you, but to inspire you: *Who the hell are you?*

If you're like I was, you might not have the answer yet—and that's okay. But it's time to start the process of discovery.

It's not an easy question. But it's the most important one you'll ever answer.

A NEW JOURNEY BEGINS

After the round table session ended, the woman approached me. Her presence was steady but gentle, like someone who knew exactly what they were doing—someone who could see beneath the surface. She introduced herself as a life coach, a title I wasn't familiar with at the time. I'd heard of counselors, therapists, mentors, and even motivational speakers, but a *life coach*? That was new.

She looked at me with the same piercing gaze she'd given me earlier and said, *"I want you to meet with me. Just you and I. Next Tuesday. Will you come?"*

Her tone wasn't forceful, but it was certain, almost as if she already knew I'd agree. And I did. There was no hesitation in my answer. I was curious, drawn to the weight of her words, the way she carried herself, and the way she had already challenged me with just one question: *"Who are you?"*

I didn't know what to expect from that meeting. What was I supposed to say? What did she want to talk about? All I knew was that something about her was different. She wasn't just talking *at* me —she was talking *to* something deep inside me, something I hadn't fully tapped into yet.

When Tuesday came, I showed up, unsure of how this was going to go. We sat down in a small, private space—just me and her. I was still a young pup, 23 years old, carrying the kind of confidence that comes from youth, but also masking a deeper uncertainty I hadn't yet faced.

For the first ten minutes, she asked me about my story—where I was from, how I got to Georgia from Maryland, and what I was doing with my life. I started sharing, thinking I was giving her the basics. But as the words started to flow, I realized that my story was more than just *facts*—it was *me*.

I told her about the struggles I'd faced getting to Georgia, about the choices I'd made, the setbacks I'd endured, and the dreams I still carried. I didn't expect her to react the way she did. Within minutes, this woman—someone who was seasoned, experienced, and probably two decades older than me—sat across from me crying.

She wiped her tears and looked at me. "You don't know how powerful you are," she said, her voice soft but full of conviction.

At first, I didn't know what to say. *Why is she crying?* I thought. This woman had just met me. I hadn't said anything extraordinary—at least, that's what I believed at the time. But there she was, crying as if I'd just spoken something profound.

"You don't see it yet," she continued. "But there's a light in you—a leadership quality that people recognize before you do. You walk into a room, and people follow you without you even trying. God has placed something powerful inside of you."

Her words shook me. I had heard similar things before, but I always brushed them off. People would say, "You're a natural leader," or "People listen when you speak," but I never took it seriously. I figured they were just being kind, or maybe they were exaggerating.

I was young. I had my mind on other things. At 23, I was trying to live my life and enjoy the world. Leadership? Influence? That sounded like too much responsibility. I wasn't ready for that because I didn't want that.

So when she looked me dead in the eye and told me, "You don't know how powerful you are"—I resisted.

I didn't want to hear it. I wasn't interested in carrying the weight of being a leader. I wanted to keep living on my terms. I thought to myself, *Why does everyone keep saying this to me? Why can't they let me be?*

But here's the thing about truth: you can resist it all you want, but it doesn't go away. It lingers. It sits with you. It echoes to you in the quiet moments.

As she kept speaking, I started to feel something shift inside me. It was uncomfortable—like a part of me was waking up that I didn't even know existed. She was right. I *didn't* know how powerful I was. I had spent so much time running from that truth, refusing to see it, because acknowledging it meant I couldn't keep living small. Acknowledging it meant I had to do something with it.

The struggle I felt that day was real. I wasn't ready to hear those words because I didn't feel ready to carry what they implied. I was still wrestling with the weight of my own insecurities, fears, and ambitions. In my mind, I was just a guy figuring life out. I was focused on the things that seemed important to me at the time: traveling, meeting people, and running a couple of small businesses I hoped would pay the bills. I wasn't thinking about purpose or influence, and I definitely wasn't thinking about my super power.

But the life coach saw something I didn't. She saw what God had placed in me—leadership, purpose, and impact. And while I couldn't fully accept it then, her words planted a seed that would eventually take root.

"You are powerful," she said again. "And when you start to see it, when you truly understand the influence you carry, everything will change."

That conversation stayed with me long after I left her presence. I couldn't stop thinking about it. At the time, I didn't have the words to describe how it made me feel. Part of me was angry— angry that she had seen something in me I wasn't ready to accept. Part of me was scared— scared of what it meant to step into that kind of responsibility. But deep down, another part of me knew she was right.

I had spent years running from who I was, hiding behind what I did. But that encounter forced me to stop, to sit with myself, and to start asking serious questions:

- Who am I?
- What has God placed in me?
- Why do people keep seeing this light in me before I see it myself?

That Tuesday session marked the beginning of something new. It was a journey that I didn't ask for, but one I needed. It first started with me understanding my identity versus my role.

WHO AM I?

For years, I confused my identity with the things I *did*. I thought I was defined by my talents, achievements, and titles. When someone asked me, *"Who are you?"* I rattled off a list of activities. But those weren't answers to the question—they were distractions. They were things I *did*, not who I *was*.

We all may fall into this trap. Society trains us to define ourselves by our roles and accomplishments. Ask someone who they are, and they'll say, "I'm an officer," "I'm a content creator," or "I'm an artist." But what happens if the title gets taken away? If you lose your job, your talent, or the role you've always played, what's left?

The challenge of answering, *"Who are you?"* when stripped of all labels is uncomfortable because it forces us to look deeper. It requires us to confront the parts of ourselves that we often ignore. The truth is, our identity isn't built on what we *do*. It's built on who we *are* at the core.

When the life coach asked me that question—*"Who are you?"*—I didn't get it at first. I couldn't separate my identity from my activities. But over time, I began to realize that *who I am* was so much more than *what I do*. My actions might change, but my identity? That's rooted in something unshakable.

As I went through this transformative journey—from that pivotal moment at 23 years old to now—I began to uncover the truth of my identity. It didn't happen overnight. It took years of prayer, reflection, mistakes, and victories. It took stripping away everything I thought I was to find the foundation of who I *am*.

So, when you ask me today, *"Who are you?"* my answer sounds a lot different:

I am a Child of God.
I am a leader.
I am a motivator.
I am a cultivator.
I am a disruptor.

These aren't roles I play or tasks I perform. They are the core of who I am, and they remain constant no matter where life takes me.

Being a child of God anchors me. Being a leader challenges me to step up. Being a motivator and cultivator means I help others grow. And being a disruptor means that I am not afraid to push boundaries and disrupt the way things are typically done.

This discovery changed everything. Once I knew *who I was*, my actions started to align with my identity. My decisions became clearer. My confidence grew—not because of what I did, but because I knew *who I belonged to* and *what I stood for*.

When you don't know who you are, you're vulnerable to anything and everything. People can define you, limit you, or mislead you, and you'll accept it because you're unsure of yourself. Society will tell you what success looks like, what happiness is, and who you *should* be— and if you're not grounded in your identity, you'll be tossed around like a leaf in the wind.

There's a saying: *"If you take someone's advice, you take their lifestyle."* I can tell you firsthand that it's true. When you don't have a strong foundation of identity, life's challenges and external influences will shake you. You'll find yourself living for the approval of others, chasing after the wrong things, and questioning your worth every time life gets hard.

I've been there. I know what it feels like to drift, unsure of my purpose, trying to find myself in the things I *do*. But let me tell you this: nothing external will ever fill the void of not knowing who you are.

What saved me—what grounded me—was my faith.

For me, discovering my identity began with understanding *whose I am*. I am God's child, and that truth anchors me no matter what life throws my way. My confidence doesn't come from my abilities, my accomplishments, or people's opinions. It comes from knowing that my identity is rooted in something greater than myself.

God will test you. Life will challenge you. Circumstances will try to shake you. But when you know *who you are* and *whose you are*, you can stand firm.

Let me share something that became clear to me over time:

- Your faith will remind you that you're not defined by your past.
- Your faith will strengthen you when you feel weak.
- Your faith will affirm you when the world tries to tear you down.

Knowing my identity in God has been the foundation of everything we've built. It's what allows me to move forward with confidence, even in the face of uncertainty.

When I was younger, I resisted this truth. I didn't want to accept the weight of leadership or influence. I wanted to live life on my terms —free, untethered, and unbothered by the expectations of others.

But as I look back now, I see the freedom in accepting who I truly am. I see the power in knowing that my identity isn't something I have to *earn*. It's something I was created with. And no person, no circumstance, no failure, and no success can take that away from me.

It's time to stop letting external influences shake you. It's time to discover your identity, anchor yourself in it, and stand firm—no matter what life brings your way.

CHAPTER 1 APPLICATION

Discovering who you truly are isn't an overnight process. It's not something you stumble upon accidentally—it's something you uncover intentionally. For many of us, the thought of "finding ourselves" can feel overwhelming, even intimidating. Where do you start? What if you don't like what you find?

The good news is that self-discovery doesn't happen in one giant leap. It happens step by step, through small, intentional actions that bring you closer to understanding the core of who you are. This process requires honesty, patience, and a willingness to dig deeper than you ever have before.

Think of it like uncovering treasure buried beneath the surface. It won't happen without effort, and the digging might get messy. But when you do the work, you'll find something priceless—clarity, confidence, and a solid foundation that no one can shake.

Here are *four* practical steps to guide you as you begin this journey of discovering your identity.

Step 1: Identify Your Truth

The first practical step in discovering your identity is deceptively simple but incredibly powerful: *write down who you are.*

Take a blank sheet of paper and write 10 things about *who you are.* Not what you do, not your job title, and not the roles you play—just *who you are* at your core. If coming up with ten feels overwhelming, start with five. Dig deep. Reflect on the values, qualities, and traits that define you beyond external labels.

For example:

- "I am a leader."
- "I am purpose driven."
- "I am resilient."
- "I am creative."

This exercise forces you to pause and think beyond the surface. You'll start to uncover pieces of yourself you may have overlooked or forgotten. Writing it down makes it real. It's a reminder you can return to when life feels shaky.

1. _____
2. _____
3. _____
4. _____
5. _____
6. _____
7. _____
8. _____
9. _____
10. _____

Step 2: Research Your Family

Your identity doesn't start and end with you. It's connected to the generations that came before you. To understand yourself more deeply, take time for family research.

Talk to your parents, grandparents, aunts, uncles—anyone you can. Ask them about their experiences:

- What were they like growing up?
- What challenges did they face?
- What habits, struggles, or successes shaped them?

As you listen to their stories, pay attention to patterns—attitudes, habits, struggles, and triumphs that might have been passed down. Maybe you'll see where your strength comes from, or where your fear of failure originates. You might notice habits you want to keep and others you need to break.

Understanding your family's history allows you to connect the dots. It gives context to the traits you carry—both the good and the bad. It helps you see how far you've come and what you're capable of overcoming.

This step isn't always easy. You may uncover things that are painful or hard to hear, but that's part of the process. You're not just discovering *where you come from*—you're deciding what to carry forward and what to leave behind.

Document what you discovered:

_____
_____
_____
_____
_____
_____
_____
_____
_____
_____
_____
_____
_____
_____
_____
_____

Step 3: Build Confidence in Your Identity

Confidence doesn't come from standing still. It comes from action —taking steps to grow, learn, and challenge yourself. Once you know who you are, you need to invest in yourself:

- Surround yourself with leaders, mentors, and experts who can pour into you.

- Read books, ask questions, and seek out opportunities to grow.
- Step out of your comfort zone and put in the work to develop your strengths.

Here's what that looks like in real life:

- If you're a musician, practice your craft. Find other musicians who can challenge you and help you grow.
- If you're a leader, seek out mentors, attend conferences, and surround yourself with people who inspire you.
- If you're a writer, don't just say you're a writer—write. Read. Ask for feedback. Keep improving.

Confidence comes from showing up, doing the work, and refusing to settle. It's not about perfection; it's about progress. The more you pour into yourself, the more confident you'll become—not just in what you do, but in who you are.

At the end of the day, your identity is your foundation. It's what allows you to stand strong, stay focused, and keep moving forward, no matter what life throws your way.

Keep investing in yourself. Be committed. And most importantly, stay true to who you are.

Document what building confidence looks like for you:

_____
_____
_____
_____
_____
_____
_____
_____
_____

_____

_____

_____

_____

_____

_____

_____

Step 4: Document Your Growth

Self-discovery isn't easy—it's messy, uncomfortable, and often painful. But it's necessary. Like a butterfly in its cocoon, transformation happens when you lean into the discomfort, not when you avoid it. You'll cry, question everything you thought you knew, and want to give up. But remember: you're not being broken, you're being prepared. When you emerge, you'll realize your growth, your struggles, and your victories were uniquely yours—and you'll finally be free to spread your wings.

Writing your journey will ground you along the way. Document your struggles, breakthroughs, and growth—it's a powerful tool for reflection and healing. Writing helps you see how far you've come and leaves a record of your truth.

And here's the truth: your story isn't just for you. Your words could inspire someone else to start their own journey of self-discovery. Whether your story becomes a blog, a book, a podcast, or stays private, it matters. Someone needs to hear your voice, see your journey, and realize they aren't alone.

You might not feel ready. You might think your story isn't big enough or good enough. But trust me—someone needs what you have to share.

So, embrace the process. Stay focused. Write it down. Celebrate your growth. You're not being destroyed—you're being prepared. The work you do now will set you free, and when you finally emerge, you'll realize just how powerful your transformation has been.

Document your growth:

_____

_____

_____

_____

_____

_____

_____

_____

_____

_____

_____

_____

_____

_____

_____

_____

_____

_____

_____

_____

Key Takeaways

If you take nothing else from this chapter, let it be this:

1. Know who you are. Your identity is the foundation of your life. If you don't know who you are, life's challenges, societal pressures, and other people's opinions will define you. Stand firm in your truth and discover who you are beyond what you do.

2. Focus on your race. Comparison steals your progress. Stop looking left and right at what others are doing and focus on your journey. Your purpose, your timing, and your growth are uniquely yours—stay in your lane and keep moving forward.

3. Build confidence in your identity. Confidence comes from action. Invest in yourself, challenge your limits, and take steps to grow. Whether it's through learning, seeking mentors, or developing your strengths, confidence is built by showing up, doing the work, and refusing to settle.

4. Document your growth. Your journey matters—not just for you, but for others who need your story to inspire their own transformation. Write it down. Reflect on your struggles, victories, and breakthroughs. Your truth is powerful, and sharing it can give someone else the courage to begin their journey.

* * *

This is your moment. When you accept the challenge—when you dig deep, write down who you are, and begin this journey—you'll find clarity, strength, and freedom like you've never known before.

So take that first step. Be honest with yourself. Write it down. Reflect. Embrace the discomfort.

This journey belongs to you, and no one else can walk it for you. But I can promise that on the other side of this process, you'll find something priceless: the power of knowing *who you truly are*.

Your transformation starts now.

CHAPTER 2
YOUR JOURNEY IS YOUR JOURNEY

Before you can take a single step forward, you need to *see* where you're going. Visualization isn't just about dreaming—it's about clarity and focus. It's about intentionally creating a picture of the life you want and believing in its possibility. When you can visualize your path, it becomes easier to stay anchored in your vision, even when challenges arise.

Each of us has a journey intricately designed by God, one that reflects His purpose and vision for our lives. No two journeys are the same. Your path, your process, and your progress are uniquely tailored to shape you into who God has called you to be.

But the challenge arises when we let comparison overshadow our confidence. We scroll through social media, see someone else's success, and feel like we're falling behind. We watch friends reach milestones we haven't yet touched and question, "What's wrong with me?" This is the trap of comparison—it sneaks in quietly and begins to rob us of joy, clarity, and peace.

The truth is simple, yet powerful: your journey is your journey—no one else's. You were never meant to look, live, or progress like anyone else. God has a specific plan for your life, and it unfolds in His timing, not according to someone else's timeline.

RUN YOUR RACE WITH SPIRITUAL BLINDERS

Life is like a race. Imagine horses at the starting line—strong, determined, and ready to run. But you'll notice something: each horse wears blinders over its eyes. Why? Because without them, they'd get distracted. The noise, the crowd, and the movement of other horses would pull their attention, and they'd veer off course.

The same principle applies to us. We need "spiritual blinders" to protect our focus. When we look to the left or right—watching what others are doing—we lose sight of where God is leading us. Comparison tempts us to measure our success based on someone else's race.

- *We see someone getting promoted* and wonder why we're still stuck in the same role.
- *We see someone else's relationship thriving* and feel like our own loneliness is a failure.
- *We see someone building a business, buying a house, or starting a family*, and we begin to doubt if we're moving forward at all.

But here's the truth: what's meant for them isn't what's meant for you. Your story is being written in God's perfect timing. When you follow Him, you're never behind—you're exactly where you need to be.

 'For I know the plans I have for you,' declares the Lord, 'plans to prosper you and not to harm you, plans to give you hope and a future.'

JEREMIAH 29:11

God's plan is personal. He doesn't rush your process, and he doesn't delay it. What looks like a delay is often preparation. What feels like being overlooked is often protection. When you trust God, you'll realize that every step—even the slow ones, even the detours— has purpose.

THE DANGER OF COMPARISON

Comparison doesn't just distract you; it distorts your vision. It tricks you into believing lies:

- "I'm not good enough."
- "I'll never catch up."
- "They're ahead, and I'm falling behind."

But the moment you start comparing, you're measuring your life with someone else's ruler—one that wasn't designed for you. You don't know their struggles, their setbacks, or the sacrifices they've made to get where they are. More importantly, their race is irrelevant to yours.

Comparison will always leave you feeling empty because it pulls your focus from God's unique work in your life. When you let go of comparison, you make space for gratitude. You begin to see the progress you've made and the blessings you already have. You recognize that God's timing is always perfect, even when it doesn't align with your expectations.

PRACTICE SELF-COMPASSION

On this journey of becoming, one of the most important lessons you'll learn is how to be kind to yourself. Self-compassion is about holding space for yourself when things don't go as planned. It's recognizing that growth is messy and that you're allowed to make mistakes along the way.

We live in a world that glorifies perfection—flawless achievements, constant success, and effortless progress. But here's the truth: your journey will not always be smooth. There will be setbacks, failures, and days when you feel like you're taking two steps back for every step forward. It's in those moments that you must practice self-compassion.

Key Reflection: *"You are becoming someone you've never been."*

Think about that for a moment. Becoming a new version of your-self—someone stronger, wiser, and more aligned with purpose—isn't supposed to be easy. It requires you to step out of your comfort zone, break old habits, and face challenges head-on. You're navigating uncharted territory, and that takes courage.

So, when you stumble—and you will—you have two choices:

1. Criticize yourself for not being "good enough" or "perfect."
2. Extend yourself grace and keep moving forward.

Too often, we default to self-criticism. We replay our mistakes, beat ourselves up for not meeting our own expectations, and let feelings of failure overshadow our progress. But let me remind you of this: *you're not supposed to have it all figured out.*

Imagine a friend coming to you, feeling defeated because something didn't work out. You wouldn't tear them down. You'd remind them of how far they've come, encourage them to keep going, and remind them that one failure doesn't define them. Why not do the same for yourself?

Self-compassion is about treating yourself with that same kindness and understanding. It's giving yourself permission to stumble, knowing that stumbling is still movement. It's pausing to say:

- "I'm learning."
- "I'm growing."
- "I'm doing the best I can, and that's enough."

The path to becoming who you're meant to be isn't paved with perfection. It's paved with progress—small, imperfect, yet beautiful steps forward.

So, when you face moments of failure, frustration, or doubt, remember this: *"Just breathe, refocus on your vision, and keep moving forward."*

Take a deep breath and remind yourself of where you're headed.

Look back at your vision board or the narrative you wrote for yourself. Let it remind you that setbacks are not the end of the story—they're just part of the process.

Here's what self-compassion looks like in action:

- Taking a break to reset when you're overwhelmed.
- Speaking words of encouragement to yourself instead of criticism.
- Celebrating the progress you've made, no matter how small it seems.

You are not falling behind. You are not failing. You are becoming. So, have compassion.

Self-compassion allows you to keep going when everything in you wants to give up. It helps you grow through challenges instead of being crushed by them. By showing yourself grace, you create space for healing, learning, and ultimately, transformation.

You won't always get it right. You won't always move as fast as you'd like. But that doesn't mean you aren't growing. Progress is still progress, even when it's messy.

So when you stumble, breathe. Refocus. And remind yourself that this is part of the process of becoming someone you've never been before. You are doing the work. You are showing up. And that's what matters most.

TRUST GOD THROUGH YOUR JOURNEY

Each of us desires to feel in control of our lives—mapping out plans, setting goals, and striving to create the future we envision. But there comes a moment when you realize that your journey and God's journey for you may not look the same. The tension between what you want and where God is leading can be uncomfortable, but it's in this tension that trust is formed. Letting go of control and allowing God to take the lead will take you further than anything you could achieve on your own.

Think of your relationship with God as a deep, unshakable connection, like the joy and excitement of a childhood crush. Remember how happy you felt when you couldn't wait to see that person? How every thought was consumed with excitement, even if it didn't make sense? That's the kind of joy and closeness a relationship with God can bring, except it doesn't fade. Even in moments of heartbreak or disappointment, God's love remains constant. He's always there, waiting patiently—even when you drift away.

The truth is, God's plans for your life will always outshine your own. You can write down your vision, create a plan, and dream big, but God sees the full picture. He knows the twists and turns of your path before you do, and He leads you with purpose. When you trust Him, He takes you further than you could have imagined. But this requires surrender—it means releasing control and allowing God to do what only He can do.

I remember working with a life coaching client who was stuck. He had degrees, accolades, and had done everything "right" by the world's standards, but nothing was moving forward. He couldn't understand why. When we talked, I told him, "You've done all that you can do. Now it's time to release control and trust God." That's a lesson so many of us face: we reach a point where our strength and effort can only carry us so far, and we need to let God step in. Sometimes, we get so focused on doing that we forget to trust.

Trusting God isn't passive—it's an active choice to lean into Him every single day. Like any relationship, your connection with God requires time and intentionality. Imagine scheduling a "date" with God—a time when you are fully present and focused. Maybe you take a walk, sit in silence, or pour out your heart in prayer. In these quiet moments, you'll hear Him more clearly. You'll begin to notice His hand in your life, whether it's through unexpected encouragement, a stranger's kind word, or a small reminder that feels like a "God smile" —a moment that reassures you He's there and He sees you.

One of the hardest parts of trusting God is understanding the difference between His timing and ours. There are seasons when it feels like nothing is happening, when doubt creeps in, and when comparison tempts you to measure your progress against someone else's. But comparison is dangerous—it distracts you from God's plan for your life. When you keep your focus on God and trust the journey He's laid out for you, you realize that you're exactly where you need to be.

There will be times when God asks you to take steps that don't make sense to anyone else. I've been there. I remember hearing God's voice telling me to move to Georgia when I was 17 years old, despite everything in my life suggesting that I should stay in Maryland. My family didn't understand; there were tears, doubts, and questions. But I trusted what God said, and within months, I had an apartment, two jobs, and a renewed sense of purpose. Later, God asked me to trust Him again and move to California—another decision that looked crazy to those around me. But every time I've followed His voice, He has smoothed the way and shown me why the move mattered.

The truth is, trusting God often requires bold obedience. It means saying "yes" when it's uncomfortable and staying still when you want to run. It means listening for His voice and following even when the path isn't clear. Along the way, doubt will show up. It always does. Doubt will come from your own insecurities, from people you trust, or from your circumstances. But when doubt creeps in, you must let your mindset fight back. Instead of focusing on what you don't know or what isn't working, anchor yourself in the truth that God is leading you.

When you trust God through the highs and lows of your journey, He shows up in ways you never expected. Sometimes, He opens a door you didn't even know was there. Other times, He closes a door you thought you needed, only to protect you from something that wasn't meant for you. Trusting God means surrendering your timeline, your plans, and your understanding of success. It's about realizing that His way is better and choosing to follow Him, no matter what it looks like.

God's journey for you will require faith, patience, and discipline. It will stretch you, refine you, and prepare you for the life He's called you to live. But here's the promise: when you trust His plan, you'll experience peace that surpasses understanding. Instead of chasing comparison or trying to control every step, you'll learn to rest in the beauty of the path He's uniquely designed for you.

So, take a deep breath. Release the pressure. Trust God. This is your journey—flawed, faithful, and full of purpose. And now, with your permission, let's begin.

CHAPTER 2 APPLICATION

Your journey is unlike anyone else's, and it's meant to be. The challenge is not just in discovering your unique path but in learning to trust God's plan for your life. When comparison tempts you to doubt, or when your timeline doesn't align with God's, it can feel overwhelming. But here's the truth: every step of your journey—whether slow, messy, or unexpected—has purpose. Trusting God means surrendering control, releasing comparison, and walking forward with faith.

Here are five practical steps to help you stay grounded, trust God's path, and fully embrace your journey.

Step 1: Visualize Your Journey

Clarity begins with vision. To stay focused on your unique path, you need to see where you're going. Take a moment to picture it—what does it look like? Who are you becoming?

1. *Create a vision board.* Find images, words, or phrases that reflect the vision God has given you. Whether physical or digital, make it a visual representation of your vision. Take a picture of it and include it below (or share the link to where it is if it's virtual).

2. *Write a short narrative describing the journey.* Be specific about the direction God has shared with you. Even though you may not know the entire plan, describe what you do know and how you plan to trust Him throughout the process.

Document your narrative below:

_____

_____

_____

_____

_____

_____

_____

_____

_____

_____

_____

_____

Step 2: Put On Your Spiritual Blinders

Comparison is a thief—it steals your joy, clarity, and peace. Like horses in a race, you need to wear "spiritual blinders" to block distractions and focus on where God is leading you.

Identify areas in your life where comparison tends to show up:

- Social media?
- Relationships?
- Career?
- Finances?

Write them down below:

1. _____
2. _____
3. _____
4. _____
5. _____

Then, write at least one intentional step you'll take to limit comparison. For example: "I will spend less time scrolling on social media" or "I will celebrate my progress without measuring it against others."

Action step(s) to limit comparison and focus forward:

_____
_____
_____
_____
_____
_____
_____
_____
_____
_____
_____

Step 3: Practice Self-Compassion

You're becoming someone you've never been, and growth is messy. You will stumble, face setbacks, and feel frustrated, but that doesn't mean you're failing. Show yourself grace—just as you would encourage a close friend.

Write down an area where you've been hard on yourself. Then reframe it with self-compassion.

Example: "I'm not where I want to be in my career." → "I'm learning and making progress, even if it's slower than I expected."

What I've been hard on myself about:

_____
_____
_____
_____

Reframed with grace:

_____
_____
_____
_____

Write one encouraging sentence you can say to yourself when you stumble.

_____
_____
_____
_____

Step 4: "Date" God and Build Trust

Your relationship with God is the foundation of your journey. Spend time with Him intentionally—praying, listening, and sharing your heart as you would with a trusted friend. Trust grows in the quiet moments of connection.

Exercise: Schedule a "date" with God this week. Choose a quiet place—a park, a quiet room, or a peaceful walk—and spend intentional time with Him. Write down what you're asking Him to reveal, what doors you need opened, and what you need clarity on.

What I'm asking God for:

_____
_____
_____
_____

What doors do I need God to close or open for me?

_____
_____
_____
_____

What is God is saying to me in this moment?

_____
_____
_____
_____

Step 5: Release Control and Trust God's Timing

Trusting God means surrendering your timeline and your plans to Him. It's understanding that His delays are often preparation, and His detours are often protection.

Think of a time when you doubted God's plan but later realized He was working things out for your good. Reflect on that moment:

1. How did you feel when things weren't going as you planned?
2. What did you learn from trusting God's timing?

Reflect on a time God worked it out:

_____

_____

_____

_____

_____

_____

_____

_____

_____

_____

_____

_____

What I learned about trusting Him:

_____

_____

_____

_____

_____

_____

_____

_____

_____

_____

_____

Write a prayer releasing control and committing to trust God with your journey:

_____

_____

_____

_____

_____

_____

_____

_____

_____

_____

_____

_____

Key Takeaways

If you take nothing from this chapter, let it be this:

1. Your journey is uniquely yours. Let go of comparison. Focus on your progress, not someone else's timeline. When you trust God, you're always exactly where you need to be.

2. Clarity comes from vision. Visualize where you're headed and stay anchored in what God has called you to do. Create reminders—like a vision board—that keep your focus forward.

3. Self-compassion fuels growth. Be kind to yourself when the journey feels hard. Remember, stumbling is still movement. Grace allows you to keep going.

4. Trust God's timing and plan. Release control and allow God to guide your steps. His delays are preparation, and His path for you will always take you further than your own.

* * *

This is your journey, and no one else can walk it for you. Comparison will try to distract you, doubt will try to stop you, and control will tempt you to force outcomes. But when you trust God, show yourself grace, and focus on His path for you, you'll see that every step—no matter how slow or challenging—is part of His perfect plan.

So, take a deep breath. Visualize where you're going. Put on your blinders. Trust God. And most importantly, keep going. Your story is unfolding beautifully, one step at a time.

CHAPTER 3
FIX THE FREQUENCY

I n life, success, purpose, and alignment with God's calling doesn't happen by accident—they require intention. The world we live in is full of distractions, influences, and voices trying to pull you in every direction. Fixing your frequency is an essential principle to staying aligned with your purpose, protecting your mind and spirit, and thriving in the life God has called you to live.

I wasn't always someone who loved conferences. I used to avoid them, feeling like they were just a long, drawn-out process. It reminded me of a concert where you show up for your favorite artist but have to sit through a lineup of opening acts you don't care about. But here's what I learned: those opening acts often drop gems—music, clarity, or insights that shift your perspective. It's the same with life. Sometimes we dismiss situations or people that don't look like part of the plan, but God uses them to refine us, challenge us, and bring us clarity.

One conference in particular changed everything for me. I heard a woman speak about guarding your gates, and the concept struck me like lightning. Guarding your gates means protecting every aspect of your life so you can stay aligned with God's will. Your gates are the openings to your mind, heart, and spirit: what you listen to, what you watch, who you allow to speak into your life, and even the words you speak over yourself. When you leave these gates unguarded, distractions and negativity sneak in, robbing you of clarity, confidence, and focus.

Your mindset is one of the most critical gates to guard. Your thoughts determine your perspective, and your perspective shapes your actions. What are you allowing to influence your mind? Are you consuming content that uplifts you, challenges you, and aligns with your purpose? Or are you letting in doubt, comparison, and negativity? You have to be intentional about what you feed your mind. The books you read, the music you listen to, the conversations you engage in—each one either fuels your growth or distracts you from it.

GET TUNED IN

To guard your gates effectively, you must also learn to fix your frequency. Think about tuning into a radio station as you drive. If you're tuned into 101.2 in one city, you might lose the signal as you cross into another county. The station starts to crackle and fill with static. To hear clearly again, you have to adjust the frequency.

Your life operates the same way. When your frequency is aligned with God—when you're in His will, spending time with Him, and pursuing His purpose—you hear Him clearly. You feel confident, focused, and unstoppable. But when you drift, the static begins. Negative influences, distractions, and doubt creep in, and the signal weakens. Fixing your frequency means checking in with God, resetting your priorities, and tuning back into His voice.

Here's the reality: some people and environments are static in your life. If you want to thrive, you need to be willing to adjust the frequency and remove what doesn't belong. Just like you wouldn't listen to a station full of static, you shouldn't allow relationships, habits, or influences to disrupt your spirit.

The company you keep matters. If you want to elevate your life, align your environment with your purpose. There's a saying: "If you want to be a millionaire, hang around millionaires." If you want to grow in your faith, spend time with people who prioritize their relationship with God. If you want to be a leader, surround yourself with leaders. Your environment shapes you—either pulling you forward or holding you back.

Here's what I've learned: successful people aren't afraid to surround themselves with others who are doing better than them. It's not about competition—it's about growth. When you're around people who challenge you, their success becomes a blueprint. You begin to think, "If they can do it, I can do it too." Your ego may want to stay in rooms where you're the smartest person, but your growth requires humility. Surround yourself with people who inspire, challenge, and push you to become the best version of yourself.

RECOGNIZING NEGATIVE INFLUENCES

Not every influence in your life deserves a seat at your table. Negative influences—whether they're people, habits, or environments—are like allergens to your spirit. If you know you're allergic to something, you don't consume it. The same principle applies here. Some relationships, conversations, and activities bring death to what God is trying to birth in your life. They stifle your growth, cause confusion, and pull you away from His purpose.

Learn to recognize the warning signs when your frequency is off:

- You feel spiritually drained or disconnected from God
- You're constantly doubting yourself or your purpose
- You feel stuck, uninspired, or overwhelmed by negativity

When you notice these signs, it's time to realign. Just as you'd avoid allergens that make you sick, you must remove anything that disrupts your peace, purpose, or connection with God. Spend time in prayer, reset your focus, and lean into God's guidance.

SET BOUNDARIES AND REALIGN

Fixing your frequency also impacts your relationships. Not everyone is meant to go with you to the next level. Some people and environments simply don't align with where God is taking you. That doesn't mean you harbor bitterness or resentment; it means you set boundaries. Boundaries protect your peace and allow you to stay focused on your purpose.

There's a story I always return to: when I realized God was calling me to move to a new season, I had to let go of relationships and environments that no longer fit. It wasn't easy. At the time, everything seemed good—life was comfortable. But deep down, I knew something wasn't right. I started asking God, "Does this align with Your plan for me?" Slowly, I began to see the cracks. I knew I couldn't ignore His voice any longer.

Sometimes, the static you feel in your life is a sign that God is asking you to adjust the frequency. It's His way of saying, "This doesn't belong here anymore." When you trust Him enough to let go, He creates space for the right people, opportunities, and blessings to flow into your life.

GUARDING YOUR GATES IS AN ACT OF TRUST

Guarding your gates and fixing your frequency isn't just about protecting yourself—it's about trusting God with your life. It's recognizing that His plan for you requires focus, intentionality, and discipline. When you stay aligned with Him, everything falls into place. Your thoughts become clearer, your relationships healthier, and your purpose stronger.

Remember this: anything outside of God's will is static—it disrupts, distorts, and distracts. So, protect your gates. Fix your frequency. Trust the process. Because when you align yourself with God's voice, you'll hear the clarity you've been searching for.

CHAPTER 3 APPLICATION

Protecting your gates and fixing your frequency is a deliberate, ongoing process. It requires you to filter out distractions, set boundaries, and align yourself with the people, habits, and environments that reflect God's purpose for your life. This activity section will guide you step-by-step to identify areas where you need to make adjustments, helping you protect your mind, spirit, and purpose.

Step 1: Identify Your Gates

Your "gates" include what you hear, see, and allow into your life. Take a moment to reflect on the areas where you've been unguarded and need more protection.

- What are you listening to? (Music, podcasts, conversations)
- What are you watching? (TV, social media, entertainment)
- Who's speaking into your life? (Friends, mentors, or negative influences)

1. Which gates in your life have been left unguarded?

_____

_____

_____

_____

2. What distractions have been pulling your focus away from God's purpose?

_____

_____

_____

_____

3. What steps can you take to guard these gates?

_____
_____
_____
_____

Step 2: Fix Your Frequency

Just like tuning a radio, you need to align yourself with God's voice. When you're not connected, you'll experience static—confusion, doubt, and lack of clarity. This exercise will help you realign.

Action Step: Identify three ways you can tune-in to God intentionally.

Examples include:

- Daily prayer
- Quiet time in nature
- Listening to worship music
- Reading Scripture

1. _____
2. _____
3. _____

Reflection Questions:

1. What are the signs that your frequency is "off"? (e.g., feeling stuck, anxious, nothing is going right in your life)

_____
_____
_____
_____

2. How does your life feel different when your frequency is aligned with God?

_____

_____

_____

_____

Step 3: Surround Yourself with the Right People

Your environment matters. The people around you can either elevate you or pull you down. To grow, you must intentionally surround yourself with people who challenge and inspire you.

Reflection Activity: List 3 people who inspire you to grow spiritually, mentally, or emotionally. These can be mentors, friends, or role models.

1. _____
2. _____
3. _____

Are there relationships in your life that drain you or cause confusion? Who do you need to set boundaries with?

_____

_____

_____

_____

_____

_____

_____

_____

_____

_____

Action Step: What is one practical boundary you need to set to protect your growth?

_____

_____

_____

_____

_____

_____

Step 4: Filter Out Negative Influences

Negative influences can disrupt your mindset and derail your progress. Just like allergens trigger physical reactions, negative influences trigger spiritual and emotional "reactions" that need to be addressed.

Activity: Write down 3 negative influences in your life (people, place, or thing).

1. _____

2. _____

3. _____

Reflection Questions:

1. What changes can you make to remove or minimize these influences?

_____

_____

_____

_____

2. How will removing these influences help you align with God's purpose for your life?

_____
_____
_____
_____

Step 5: Set Spiritual Boundaries and Realign with God

Sometimes, fixing your frequency means stepping back from what feels familiar and reconnecting with God. This is where your spiritual discipline and boundaries come in.

Action Step: Schedule a "date" with God this week. Pick a time and place where you can reflect, pray, and realign. Write out your plan:

Date/Time: _____ Location: _____

What will you do? (e.g., pray, journal, meditate on Scripture):

_____
_____
_____
_____

Reflection:

After spending time with God, what did you hear or feel? Write it down.

_____
_____
_____
_____

_____

_____

_____

_____

_____

_____

Key Takeaways

If you take nothing else from this chapter, let it be this:

1. Guard your gates. Be intentional about what you allow into your mind, heart, and spirit. Protect your focus and clarity.

2. Fix your frequency. Stay spiritually connected to God by tuning into His voice through prayer, reflection, and time in His presence.

3. Align your environment. Surround yourself with people and influences that elevate you, challenge you, and align with your purpose.

4. Remove negative influences. Anything that distracts you from God's purpose is static—identify it, filter it out, and realign with Him.

* * *

You don't have to live surrounded by distractions, negativity, or confusion. You can guard your gates, fix your frequency, and align yourself with the purpose God has for you. Take these steps seriously —write them down, reflect on your progress, and trust that God is guiding you every step of the way. Your transformation starts now.

THE MILK HAS GONE BAD

There comes a time in life when something that once served you—whether a relationship, job, mindset, or season—has reached its expiration date. Like spoiled milk, holding on too long can make you sick. It becomes toxic to your mental, emotional, spiritual, and even physical well-being. Recognizing when something has expired is easy. The difficult part is letting go because it's essential to your growth, freedom, and purpose.

I'll never forget a conversation I had with a successful entrepreneur named Paul. I met him during a fashion show Drew and I hosted at the L2 Lounge in Georgetown, DC for our clothing brand. I typically ask those who are doing better in life, "What's the secret to success?" Paul looked me in the eyes and said, "Jonathan, the best advice I can give you is this: Once something isn't fun anymore, walk away. When it's no longer fun, it becomes work—and no one really wants to work. Things will require effort, but they should still carry joy."

His words stuck with me because they were profound and practical. When the joy fades, and what once energized you begins to drain you, it's time to take a step back. That principle applies to every area of your life: relationships, work, habits, and even the way you think. Holding on when something has expired doesn't just hold you back—it makes you sick.

RECOGNIZING WHEN IT'S TIME TO LET GO

So, how do you know when something has reached its expiration date? For starters, you'll feel it in your spirit before you see it in your circumstances. You'll notice signs:

- *The joy fades:* What once brought you excitement now feels heavy. You dread showing up.

- *Stagnation sets in:* You're no longer growing. The relationship, job, or mindset feels repetitive and lifeless.

- *It drains you:* You feel emotionally, spiritually, and even physically exhausted from holding on.

- *People notice:* Friends or loved ones ask, "Are you okay?" because they see something is off.

- *You're forcing it:* You're trying to make it work when, deep down, you know it's not meant for you.

It's like drinking spoiled milk. You take a sip and instantly regret it, yet sometimes, you convince yourself to keep trying because you don't want to waste it. But the more you drink, the sicker you get. The same is true for staying in expired relationships, jobs, or thought patterns— you're poisoning yourself by refusing to let go.

NAVIGATING THE EMOTIONAL CHALLENGES OF LETTING GO

Letting go isn't easy, especially when you've invested time, energy, and love into something or someone. It feels like grieving, and in many ways, it is. But here's what I've learned: you must separate your emotions from the truth. In life we need to make choices that break our hearts, but heal our soul.

- *Logically*, you know what's not working. The relationship isn't growing, the job isn't fulfilling, or the mindset isn't serving you.
- *Spiritually*, God may be showing you that this isn't where you belong. Maybe He never cleared you to be here, and now He's nudging you toward something better.

But your emotions? They hold on for dear life. They remind you of the good moments—the laughs, the comfort, and the familiarity. They tell you to stay because "What if I miss it?" or "What if I don't find anything better?"

Letting go isn't about what you're losing—it's about what you're making room for. When God calls you to let go, He's preparing you for something greater. Holding on to expired things doesn't just keep you stuck; it keeps you from the blessings waiting on the other side of your obedience.

EMBRACE CHANGE

Change is uncomfortable, but it's necessary. When you resist it, you end up clinging to what's familiar, even when it no longer fits. It's like wearing shoes that are too small—they hurt, but you refuse to take them off because you're used to them.

Tupac Shakur, one of the greatest cultural icons of our time, accomplished more in six years than most do in a lifetime. He understood that life is short and time is precious. You don't know how much time you have, but you can't waste it holding on to things that no longer serve you.

When you let go of what's expired, you make room for:

- Peace that surpasses understanding
- Joy that comes from living in alignment with God's purpose
- Growth that stretches you into a stronger, wiser version of yourself

- Opportunities that exceed your expectations

Staying where you don't belong comes at a cost. You'll feel the weight of it spiritually, emotionally, and physically. The longer you hold on, the more it steals your peace. God didn't design you to live in bondage to expired seasons. He created you to thrive, to grow, and to make an impact.

THE PROCESS OF LETTING GO

So, how do you let go when you're afraid of what's next? You start by being honest with yourself and with God. Write down the reality of your situation:

- *Where did this start?* What drew you to this relationship, job, or mindset?
- *Where are you now?* Is it meeting your wants and needs, or is it holding you back?
- *Where do you want to be?* What does freedom look like?

Give yourself time to evaluate. Pray for clarity, and ask God to show you the truth. Be prepared—He will show you. Your job is to listen, trust, and act.

Letting go is never easy, but holding on to what's expired may cost you your peace, progress, and purpose. So, choose freedom. Choose growth. Choose the future God has already prepared for you.

Spoiled milk doesn't satisfy you or anyone else; it corrupts everything around it. Don't hesitate. Toss it out. Make room for what's fresh, what's next, and what's divinely yours.

If the milk has gone bad, throw it away.

CHAPTER 4 APPLICATION

Letting go of something that no longer serves you is not always easy. It's human nature to hold on to what feels familiar, even when we know it's expired. But the truth is, holding on to expired things keeps us stuck. Like drinking spoiled milk, it can make us sick—mentally, emotionally, spiritually, and even physically.

This process requires honesty, self-reflection, and trust. You must be willing to acknowledge the signs, let go of what's expired, and step into the life God has for you. Remember: you can't receive what's next if your hands are still full of what's expired.

Here are five steps to help you navigate this process.

Step 1: Identify What's Expired

The first step is recognizing what no longer serves you. Take an honest look at your life—relationships, jobs, habits, mindsets, and environments. Ask yourself:

- Is this adding value to my life, or is it draining me?
- Do I feel fulfilled, or do I feel stuck and unmotivated?
- Am I holding onto this out of fear, guilt, or comfort?

Make two lists: In the first list, write what's currently serving you and bringing you joy. In the other list, write what feels expired, feels toxic, or no longer aligns with where you're going.

What still serves me?

1. _____
2. _____
3. _____
4. _____
5. _____

What feels expired, feels toxic, or no longer aligns?

1. _____
2. _____
3. _____
4. _____
5. _____

Step 2: Recognize the Warning Signs

When milk spoils, it gives clear signs; it smells bad, tastes sour, and looks off. The same is true for the things in our lives that have expired.

Common Signs:

- You feel drained, unmotivated, or unfulfilled.
- You keep making excuses for why you're still in the situation.
- Your health, relationships, or mental well-being are suffering.
- You sense God prompting you to let go, but you resist.

Reflection Question:

What are the warning signs in your current situation? Write them down. Be specific and honest.

_____
_____
_____
_____
_____
_____
_____

Step 3: Separate Emotion from Logic

Letting go is difficult because emotions get in the way. You might feel fear, guilt, or sadness about ending a relationship, leaving a job, or releasing a mindset. But emotions can cloud the truth.

To gain clarity, focus on the spiritual and logical perspective:

- *Spiritual*: Is this aligned with God's plan for my life? Have I prayed and sought His guidance?

- *Logical*: Is this adding value, or am I staying for comfort? What are the consequences of holding on?

- *Reflection Activity*: Write out both perspectives. Separate the emotion so you can see the bigger picture.

Spiritual Perspective:

_____
_____
_____
_____
_____
_____
_____

Logical Perspective:

_____
_____
_____
_____
_____
_____

Step 4: Create a Transition Plan

Once you've identified what's expired, it's time to prepare to let go. You don't have to rush the process, but you do need to start moving forward.

- **Pray**: Ask God to give you peace, clarity, and direction.

- **Plan**: Write down what steps you need to take to let go—whether it's having a tough conversation, applying for a new job, or releasing an old mindset.

- **Act**: Start small. Progress, not perfection, is the goal.

Activity:

What steps will you take to transition out of this expired situation? List them here:

1. _____
2. _____
3. _____
4. _____
5. _____

Step 5: Embrace the New and Trust God's Timing

Letting go creates space for God to bring new opportunities, relationships, and growth into your life. But you must trust His timing and purpose.

Reflection Questions:

- What do I believe God is preparing me for?
- How can I embrace this change with faith instead of fear?

_____

_____

_____

_____

_____

_____

_____

_____

Activity: Write a prayer or declaration of trust as you step into the new.

_____

_____

_____

_____

_____

_____

_____

_____

Key Takeaways

If you take nothing else from this chapter, let it be this:

1. Recognize what's expired. When something no longer serves you, it's time to let go. Holding onto expired things keeps you stuck and unhealthy.

2. Look for the warning signs. Pay attention to the ways God shows you it's time to move on—through discomfort, frustration, or a lack of fulfillment.

3. Trust God and separate emotions from truth. Letting go is hard, but God's plans for you are greater than anything you're holding onto.

4. *Take intentional steps forward.* Create a plan, pray for clarity, and trust that letting go makes room for God's best in your life.

Letting go isn't the end; it's the beginning of something better. Trust that when you release what's expired, God will provide what's fresh, new, and aligned with His purpose for your life. You deserve to thrive, not just survive.

THE BREAK-UP

I n life, there comes a time when everything slows down. You're not moving forward as quickly as you'd like, and nothing seems to be happening. These moments of pause—the breaks—are often uncomfortable. The world tells us that we should always be in motion, always "hustling" and chasing the next big thing. So, when life slows down, it can feel frustrating, like you're stuck or falling behind.

When God slows things down in your life, it's because He's setting you up for what's coming next. A break is an invitation to pause, reflect, and realign yourself with His purpose. It's a time to let go of distractions, focus on growth, and prepare for the new season ahead.

USE YOUR BREAK WISELY

Many people mistake breaks for "down time" and use them to disconnect without purpose—scrolling through social media, binge-watching shows, or filling their lives with distractions. But breaks are far more valuable when you use them intentionally.

Breaks are a time to grow. Growth doesn't happen when everything is easy or comfortable; it happens when you're stretched. It happens when you step back, surrender control, and allow God to

move in ways you cannot. It's in these pauses that you can take a step
back and ask yourself the hard questions:

- Why am I feeling stuck?
- What is draining me emotionally, spiritually, or mentally?
- What habits, relationships, or mindsets do I need to let
  go of?
- What is God asking me to do in this season?

These questions are uncomfortable because they force you to
confront truths you may have been avoiding. But the answers are key
to unlocking what comes next.

During times of rest or pause, your mindset must shift. Instead of
seeing the break as a setback, see it as an opportunity. God isn't
punishing you—He's positioning you. The question is: *Will you trust
Him enough to sit still?*

I remember going through a period like this. I had just gotten out
of jail, and I was trying to do everything— write a book, start a
podcast, life coach, and build a business. I was doing the most because
I thought "doing" was the answer. But God told me to stop. I wasn't
ready yet. My spirit was broken, and my mind was cluttered with
distractions. *So, I sat still.*

I went on a 17-day water fast, deleted all of my social media
accounts, and changed my phone number. I deleted pictures, videos,
and conversations that were no longer serving me in order to spend
time alone with God. It was hard—no food, no distractions— just me
and Him. But in that stillness, I realized how much noise I had been
letting into my life. I wasn't feeding my spirit; I was feeding my stress.

That break changed everything. I started to hear God's voice more
clearly. My heart felt lighter, my mind sharper, and my purpose clearer.
When the fast ended, God led me to California, where I thought I'd be
for a quick visit. Instead, I stayed for almost a year. That season of
stillness prepared me for what was next—new opportunities, clarity,
and purpose that I couldn't have imagined before.

In fact, every time I've trusted God in a transition—whether it was moving to a new city, walking away from relationships, or letting go of control, He has opened doors I never could have opened myself. It's not easy, and it doesn't always make sense at first. But when you walk in obedience, everything starts to align. You'll know you're ready for the next phase when:

- Your mindset shifts from fear to faith
- Your conversations reflect growth and clarity
- Your decisions align with God's purpose, not your comfort

You'll feel it in your spirit. The places that once drained you will no longer satisfy you. The distractions that once held you back will no longer appeal to you. And the fear that once kept you stuck will be replaced with confidence in God's plan.

LEARN THE LESSON

Every break comes with lessons, but you must be willing to look for them. If you feel challenged or uncomfortable, that's a sign you're being stretched. God uses these pauses to refine you, strengthen you, and prepare you for the next phase of your journey.

Write everything down. Document the dreams, the visions, and the quiet whispers you hear in prayer. Pay attention to the conversations you have, the people who pour into you, and the shifts happening around you. These are all clues—signs that God is at work, even when you can't see the full picture yet.

God isn't breaking you; He's preparing you. It's God's way of saying, "You're not ready yet, but I'm getting you there."

So, if you're in a season of waiting, don't fight it. Don't rush it. Use this time to grow, reflect, and reset. Let go of what's distracting you, and focus on the God who is preparing you. When the break ends, and God calls you forward, you'll be ready to step into the life He has been preparing for you all along.

CHAPTER 5 APPLICATION

Breaks are not wasted time; they are sacred opportunities for growth, alignment, and preparation. If you approach them intentionally, you can use this season of waiting to uncover lessons, shift your mindset, and build a strong foundation for what's coming next. This workbook will guide you step-by-step to reflect on your break, embrace the process, and move forward with clarity.

Step 1: Identify Why You Need the Break

In order to make the most of your pause, you first need to understand why you're in this season. Take a moment to reflect on your current situation and answer these questions honestly:

What is draining me emotionally, mentally, or spiritually right now?

_____

_____

_____

_____

_____

_____

_____

Where am I forcing something that no longer feels aligned with my purpose?

_____

_____

_____

_____

_____

_____

_____

What habits, relationships, or situations am I holding onto that God may be asking me to let go of?

_____

_____

_____

_____

_____

_____

_____

Write down any patterns, feelings, or realizations that stand out to you as you reflect. These are areas God may be calling you to address during this break.

_____

_____

_____

_____

_____

_____

_____

Step 2: Realign Your Focus

During a break, your mindset must shift. Instead of seeing it as a setback, use this time to realign yourself with God's plan. Write down three things you want to focus on during this season of stillness.

1. _____
2. _____
3. _____

Now, take a moment to pray over this list. Ask God to help you let go of distractions and focus on what He's preparing for you.

Step 3: Listen for God's Voice

The break is an opportunity to get quiet and hear what God is saying to you. Use this space to reflect on recent dreams, moments, or feelings that may be guiding you:

Have I had any dreams, visions, or "God whispers" lately that stood out to me?

_____
_____
_____
_____
_____
_____
_____
_____
_____
_____

What scripture, song, or encouraging words have brought me peace or clarity?

_____
_____
_____
_____
_____
_____
_____
_____

Write these down and keep them close. These moments of clarity may reveal what God is preparing you for.

Step 4: Take Proactive Steps

Even in the waiting, you can stay productive by building yourself up spiritually, mentally, and physically. Write down practical actions you can take to prepare for what's coming:

Spiritually (prayer, scripture, fasting):

_____

_____

_____

_____

_____

_____

_____

Mentally (journaling, reading, speaking with mentors):

_____

_____

_____

_____

_____

_____

_____

Physically (rest, exercise, creating healthy routines):

_____

_____

_____

_____

_____

_____

_____

Now, commit to one small action you can take today to move closer to your goals:

_____
_____
_____
_____
_____

Step 5: Reflect on the Lessons of Your Break

At the end of each day or week, take a moment to reflect on what you're learning during this break. Write down:

What lessons is God teaching me in this season?

_____
_____
_____
_____
_____
_____
_____

How am I growing spiritually, mentally, or emotionally?

_____
_____
_____
_____
_____
_____
_____
_____

What am I letting go of, and what am I making space for?

_____

_____

_____

_____

_____

_____

_____

Key Takeaways

If you take nothing else from this chapter, let it be this:

1. Your break is not wasted time. It's a period of preparation and alignment for the life God is calling you to.

2. Growth requires stillness. Use this season to reflect, listen, and surrender your plans to God.

3. Stay proactive. Focus on spiritual growth, personal development, and creating healthy habits.

4. Document the journey. Write down lessons, dreams, and breakthroughs. This will remind you of how far you've come and help you move forward with confidence.

This is your preparation season. Be still, trust God, and allow Him to prepare you for what's next. *"Be still, and know that I am God."* – Psalm 46:10 (NIV)

THERE IS A WEIGHT IN THE WAIT

There comes a time in all of our lives when we are forced to wait. It might be for a job, an opportunity, healing, restoration, or even direction. Waiting can feel heavy—like carrying a weight that you don't know how to put down. The process can feel uncomfortable, frustrating, and endless. But here's the reality: there is purpose in the wait. There's something God wants you to see, learn, and become before He opens the door to what's next.

I learned this firsthand on a weekend trip to North Carolina. On the way there, I started feeling a sharp pain on my side. At first, I brushed it off as nothing. I told myself it would pass, like a cramp or random ache. But as the night went on, the pain crept up toward my chest. By the next morning, it was worse—*still*, I ignored it. I was laughing, eating, and moving as if nothing was wrong. But by the third night, the pain became unbearable. It felt like a thousand feet stomping on my chest, and I finally had no choice but to go to the hospital.

The doctors ran every test—EKGs, bloodwork, x-rays—while I lay in the hospital bed, barely able to move without feeling that intense pressure. I remember looking up to God and saying, "God, I don't know what this is, but I trust You. I can't do this alone." At that moment, in the waiting room of uncertainty, I realized something powerful: the weight wasn't just the physical pain; it was the mental and emotional challenge of waiting for answers.

The doctor came back after what felt like hours and said, "We want to rule out a few things. You could have blood clots in your lungs." I rebuked that immediately. I refused to let fear creep in or to create a negative narrative that wasn't mine to carry. That's one of the first lessons I learned about waiting: *rebuke anything negative that tries to take root in your mind or spirit.* You can't control what others say, but you can control what you believe.

A little later, the doctor returned with another possible explanation: shortness of breath. Again, I pushed that aside. "God, whatever this is, I trust You." Finally, after more tests, the doctor told me I had pneumonia. And you know what? That was a relief. It wasn't what I had feared, and the treatment was simple—antibiotics for a week. By the third day of medication, I was back to normal. But the peace I had in that hospital room wasn't because of what the doctor said—it was because I had chosen to trust God in the waiting.

THE PURPOSE IN THE WAIT

Most of us view waiting as inactivity. We associate waiting with sitting still and doing nothing. But waiting on God is anything but passive. *Waiting is active; it's faith in action.* Waiting requires trust, obedience, and discipline. It's in the waiting that God prepares you for what's next.

Imagine a farmer planting seeds. The seed doesn't sprout into a full plant overnight. The farmer has to wait. During that waiting period, there's growth happening beneath the surface that no one can see. The soil is nourishing the seed, the roots are forming, and everything is being prepared for the harvest. But the seed must also be planted in good soil— soil that's rich, healthy, and ready to receive it. In the same way, our hearts must be good ground, ready to receive what God is planting within us.

Patience is what allows the blessing to fully develop. If the farmer pulled the seed out of the ground too soon, it wouldn't survive. The same goes for you: if you rush the process, you'll miss the full miracle. There's a weight in the wait because what God is preparing for you requires you to be ready to carry it. This requires that you trust God's timing.

One of the hardest parts of waiting is not knowing how long it will last. Will it be days? Months? Years? That uncertainty can make you want to take matters into your own hands. But I've learned the hard way that moving before God tells you to move only creates more problems.

When I was in California, I kept trying to make things happen on my own. I was chasing opportunities, forcing situations, and getting frustrated when nothing worked out. Finally, God told me to sit still. At first, I resisted. Sitting still felt like I was wasting time. But eventually, I surrendered. I stopped forcing things and started listening to God's direction. And that's when everything began to shift.

God isn't asking you to do nothing—He's asking you to trust Him. Waiting is about surrendering your plans, your timeline, and your understanding of how things should look. It's about saying, "God, I don't know what's next, but I know You do."

The waiting season is where growth happens. It's where your faith is strengthened, your character is refined, and your vision becomes clearer. It's where God strips away distractions, bad habits, and relationships that aren't meant to go with you into the next season.

While you're waiting:

- *Spend time in prayer.* Let God speak to you and show you what He wants you to learn.

- *Write it down.* Write your thoughts, prayers, dreams, and reflections. Documenting the process helps you see how far you've come.

- *Stay disciplined.* Don't let frustration or impatience pull you

out of alignment. Stay focused on what God has called you
to do.

- *Trust the process.* Even when it doesn't make sense, believe
that God is working all things together for your good.

THE BLESSING OF THE WAIT

The weight you feel during the wait is preparing you to carry the
blessing that's coming. Think about it— if you were handed everything you wanted today, would you be ready for it? Would you know
how to steward it? Sometimes, God keeps you in the waiting season
because He's growing your capacity. The miracle isn't just what
happens at the end of the wait. The miracle is who you become in the
process. You become stronger, wiser, and more prepared for the opportunities God has for you.

I often think of waiting like the game "Red Light, Green Light."
God says, "Red light"—you stop. You don't move, even if it feels
uncomfortable. Then God says, "Green light"—you go. You don't hesitate, you don't question, you just move forward in obedience. The key
is knowing God's voice well enough to discern when it's time to move
and when it's time to wait.

Let me remind you of this: you are not being punished by the wait
—you are being prepared. God's timing is perfect. He sees the full
picture, and He knows exactly when to release the blessing you've
been waiting for.

So, what should you do in the meantime?

Keep *showing up*.
Keep *praying*.
Keep *listening*.
Keep *trusting*.

And when the time is right, God will open the door. And when He does, you'll be ready to walk through it.

Waiting is hard, but it's worth it. Don't give up. The blessing is coming. The miracle is on the way. And when it comes, you'll realize that the weight you carried in the wait was preparing you for the life you were meant to live.

 Wait for the Lord; be strong and take heart and wait for the Lord.

PSALM 27:14 (NIV)

CHAPTER 6 APPLICATION

Periods of waiting can feel heavy, but they are not wasted. In this workbook, you'll reflect on your waiting seasons, identify areas where you need patience, and uncover the growth God is calling you into. This isn't about sitting idly—this is about preparing, trusting, and shifting your mindset to embrace the process God is using to shape you.

Step 1: Identify Your Waiting Season

Take a moment to reflect on your life right now. What areas feel like you are in a holding pattern? It could be a job, a relationship, healing, or a personal goal. Write down the specific area(s) where you feel like you're waiting.

What am I currently waiting for?

_____
_____
_____
_____
_____
_____
_____

What emotions come up when I think about this waiting season?

_____
_____
_____
_____
_____
_____
_____

Step 2: Reflect on Past Breakthroughs

Sometimes, the best way to stay encouraged in the wait is to look back at the times God showed up for you before. Think about a past waiting season in your life—how did God come through for you, even when you didn't see it at first?

What is one time I had to wait for something, and what happened?

_____

_____

_____

_____

_____

_____

_____

_____

_____

_____

_____

_____

What did I learn from that experience?

_____

_____

_____

_____

_____

_____

_____

_____

_____

_____

_____

_____

Step 3: Write a Letter to God

Use this step to talk directly to God about your waiting season. Write
a letter sharing your frustrations, hopes, and questions. Be honest
about how you feel, but also ask Him to help you trust His timing. An
example has been included below to get you started.

Dear God,

*Thank You for working in my life, even when I don't
see it. Help me to trust You in this season of waiting.*

Step 4: Take Action During the Wait

Waiting doesn't mean doing nothing; it's about preparing for what's coming. What can you do right now to stay proactive and keep growing, even while you wait? Write down 3 action steps you can take during this time.

Examples:

- Spend 10 minutes a day praying or reading Scripture.
- Start journaling my thoughts and dreams.
- Invest in learning something new that aligns with my goals.

What are 3 small, intentional steps I can take while I wait?

1. _____
2. _____
3. _____

Step 5: Recognize the Growth

Your waiting season is where God refines you. It's where He stretches your faith, sharpens your character, and prepares you for the blessing ahead. Take a moment to reflect on how this waiting season is shaping you.

How is this season teaching me patience, trust, or discipline?

_____
_____
_____
_____
_____
_____
_____

What qualities or habits is God growing in me during this time?

_____

_____

_____

_____

_____

_____

_____

_____

_____

Key Takeaways

If you take nothing else from this chapter, let it be this:

1. Your waiting season is not wasted. God is working in ways you can't yet see.

2. Be active in the wait. Focus on preparation, prayer, and trusting God's timing.

3. Shift your perspective. The weight of waiting is where growth, healing, and clarity happen.

* * *

When it feels heavy, remember this: God isn't punishing you—He's preparing you. Every day you choose to trust Him, you're one step closer to the breakthrough He's promised. Keep the faith, stay the course, and let God use this time to refine you. *"Be still before the Lord and wait patiently for Him."* – Psalm 37:7 (NIV)

THE POWER OF "NAH"

L earning to say "nah" is crucial because your life and your purpose are precious and must be protected. Every choice you make either moves you closer to or further away from your God-given purpose. Think of life as governed by certain laws designed to keep you safe and aligned with your destiny. Just like laws in society, such as traffic laws, exist to prevent harm and maintain order, your personal boundaries—your ability to say "nah"—serve a similar purpose in your life.

Imagine driving while distracted or under the influence: there are severe consequences. Similarly, when you fail to say "nah" to things that don't align with your purpose, the results can be equally damaging—mentally, emotionally, and spiritually. Saying "nah" allows you to maintain focus, stay safe, and ensure that you're moving in harmony with your purpose.

RECOGNIZING WHAT'S DRAINING VS. UPLIFTING

To stay aligned, you must learn to identify people, places, and situations that uplift versus those that drain you. Initially, it might not be obvious, especially if you've become accustomed to certain patterns or environments. But if you regularly question why you're stuck or repeating negative patterns, chances are you're surrounded by draining influences.

For instance, if you're meant to write a book or pursue an important goal, spending every weekend at social events is not productive. It might feel enjoyable temporarily, but it's ultimately draining your purpose-driven energy. On the other hand, being around people who inspire you, attending events relevant to your goals, and engaging in meaningful conversations provide upliftment and forward momentum. Remember, your spirit knows what's genuinely beneficial. Trust that internal guidance and act accordingly.

DISCONNECT AND SET BOUNDARIES

Here are two practical steps that you can incorporate into your lifestyle:

First, be completely real with yourself about what you need. Disconnecting from hindering influences begins with honesty. Don't focus on pleasing others or accommodating their desires; prioritize what your life requires for growth and alignment.

Second, decide whether conversations are necessary. Sometimes direct conversations help bring closure or clarity; other times, they might create confusion or conflict. Trust your instincts and spiritual discernment. If a relationship or situation no longer serves your highest purpose, it's perfectly acceptable to quietly remove yourself. Silence itself is a powerful boundary.

Consider when you're ready to leave a job. Often, the employer suddenly offers more money or benefits as you're about to leave. However, once you've decided to move on, stay firm in your decision. No explanation is necessary. Your reason for moving forward is sufficient. Maintain that same confidence when setting boundaries in relationships and opportunities. If they're not aligned with your purpose, confidently and respectfully say "nah."

THE IMPACT OF SAYING "NAH"

Saying "nah" can bring guilt or discomfort, especially when relationships or familiar routines are involved. But emotions must be balanced by logical and spiritual discernment. Consider professional athletes who leave teams that don't support their growth to join those that do. They recognize their value and understand when an environment no longer serves their progression. It's crucial to recognize your worth and not feel guilty about moving towards environments and relationships that support your potential.

If someone around you isn't helping you grow or, worse, drains your energy while falsely claiming to uplift you, step back. Often, those who claim loudest to contribute positively to your life are the ones most in need of growth themselves. Don't feel guilty for stepping away from that dynamic; it's necessary for your growth and alignment.

The benefit of saying "nah" to things that don't serve your highest purpose is freedom to elevate without unnecessary burdens. Imagine life as an elevator with a maximum weight limit. Allowing too many draining influences inside will prevent you from rising. Every time you say "nah" to negativity, distractions, and toxic relationships, you're keeping your elevator free to ascend toward your goals and higher purpose.

You can only reach your highest potential when you release what doesn't belong. Protect your boundaries fiercely. Don't permit extra weight—unnecessary obligations, toxic relationships, distractions—to hold you down. The clearer your boundaries, the lighter you'll feel, and the easier it becomes to achieve your purpose.

BALANCING RELATIONSHIPS

Balancing relationships means more than just managing your social calendar—it's about discerning alignment. Every connection you maintain either pulls you forward or holds you back. And while it's not always obvious at first, over time, people show you who they are—and more importantly, how they impact your purpose.

When you enter a new relationship—whether romantic, professional, platonic, or spiritual—there's always a season of discovery. During the first three to six months, you're learning the rhythm of that relationship. You're observing patterns, listening closely to how they speak to your vision, and watching how they respond when you grow. Do they celebrate your elevation or compete with it? Do they stretch you or suppress you?

This evaluation period is not about judgment—it's about stewardship. You are responsible for protecting the calling on your life, and that includes auditing who has access to it.

One of the most overlooked dynamics in relationship management is understanding the difference between high-maintenance and low-maintenance relationships:

- *High-maintenance* relationships are emotionally expensive. They constantly require reassurance, attention, or rescue. These connections often leave you drained, confused, or second-guessing yourself. They don't just demand your time —they demand your identity.

- *Low-maintenance* relationships, on the other hand, are grounded in mutual trust, respect, and independence. These are the people you can go weeks without talking to and pick right back up like nothing changed. They inspire you to grow, and they don't feel threatened by your evolution. Instead, they water your roots and celebrate your bloom.

Once you've identified the difference, you can make wise choices about how you engage. High-maintenance doesn't always mean "cut off," but it does mean boundary up. You don't owe constant availability to anyone. You owe yourself clarity, peace, and alignment.

And this is where your "nah" becomes powerful. Saying no isn't rejection—it's protection. It's choosing purpose over pressure. It's preserving the space you need to flourish without apology.

Protect your peace like it's sacred—because it is. Your purpose

depends on it. And anyone who threatens it, intentionally or uninten-
tionally, must be placed accordingly. Love them, pray for them, but
don't give them a seat at the table of your destiny if they're not
bringing nourishment.

Balancing relationships isn't always easy, but it's essential. Every
"yes" to someone else is a "nah" to something else. So choose wisely.
Honor the relationships that honor your growth. Set limits where
needed. And remember—sometimes your greatest breakthrough is
waiting on the other side of a boundary you were afraid to set.

CHAPTER 7 APPLICATION

Learning to harness the power of "nah" is one of the most empowering and crucial skills you can develop. Saying no isn't about being negative or dismissive; it's about protecting your peace, purpose, and potential. Let's explore this practically and intentionally.

Step 1: Identify Your "Nah" Moments

Think about the recent moments when you felt drained, conflicted, or unsettled by something you agreed to but later regretted. Write down 3-5 instances:

1. _____
2. _____
3. _____
4. _____
5. _____

Next, reflect on why you initially said yes instead of no. Was it pressure, obligation, fear of conflict, or fear of missing out? Understanding your triggers helps you recognize future moments when saying "nah" is necessary.

Step 2: Evaluate Your Relationships and Commitments

Start by making two lists. Write down three relationships/ activities under each category.

Uplifting and Supportive Relationships/Activities:

1. _____
2. _____
3. _____

Draining or Distracting Relationships/Activities:

1. _____
2. _____
3. _____

For each item on the "draining" list, write down a clear reason why it's time to distance yourself or say "nah" moving forward.

_____
_____
_____
_____
_____
_____
_____
_____
_____

Step 3: Practice Saying "Nah"

Think about a situation or request you anticipate receiving soon— something that will challenge your commitment to your purpose. Write a simple, respectful script you can use to say no firmly yet kindly:

_____
_____
_____
_____
_____
_____
_____
_____

Practice saying this out loud. How does it feel? Do you feel confident, nervous, or empowered? Write down your reflection:

_____
_____
_____
_____
_____
_____
_____

Step 4: Overcome Guilt and Discomfort

Saying no can sometimes create feelings of guilt. Identify the specific emotions or thoughts that come up when you imagine saying no to someone:

1. _____
2. _____
3. _____

Now, challenge each thought by writing a truthful, affirming statement next to it.

For example:

- Guilt: "They will be upset with me."
- Affirmation: "My peace and purpose matter, and healthy relationships respect boundaries."

Write your affirmations below:

1. _____
2. _____
3. _____

Step 5: Set Healthy Boundaries

Boundaries are guidelines to protect your well-being and growth. Write down at least three personal boundaries you commit to setting moving forward:

1. _____
2. _____
3. _____

How will you communicate these boundaries clearly?

_____
_____
_____
_____
_____
_____
_____
_____
_____
_____

Key Takeaways

If you take nothing else from this chapter, let it be this:

1. Saying "nah" is essential for aligning with your purpose and maintaining your peace.

2. Clearly identifying what's draining versus uplifting helps you make empowered decisions.

3. Guilt may arise initially, but *affirming your worth and purpose* helps manage discomfort.

4. Boundaries are necessary for your growth; define and communicate them clearly.

* * *

You're ready to embrace the power of "nah." Protect your space, guard your gates, and honor your purpose.

CHAPTER 8
CHAMPAGNE VICTORY LAP

O ne of my favorite athletes is a renowned boxer. He's undefeated, living a luxurious lifestyle many dream of, yet his work ethic remains unmatched. Despite his wealth and undefeated status, he trains with the hunger and urgency of someone who's just starting out. Even without an upcoming fight, he works tirelessly, maintaining discipline as if he's still striving for his first victory.

This relentless approach is a powerful lesson in avoiding complacency. When we achieve significant milestones, it's easy to feel entitled to rest and indulge in comfort. However, true sustained success requires continuous effort and adaptability. We must keep evolving, learning, and growing, staying ahead of trends and technological advancements. Just as banking systems shift toward digital platforms and artificial intelligence revolutionizes industries, we too must continually reinvent ourselves.

CELEBRATING YOUR WINS WITHOUT LOSING MOMENTUM

It's important to pause and celebrate what you've accomplished—but even more important to understand why you're celebrating and what's next. Wins are not just finish lines; they're checkpoints. They remind you that progress is possible, that the grind was worth it, and that your vision is not in vain. But they're not the destination.

When you celebrate, let it be a moment of reflection, not retirement. Take the time to acknowledge how far you've come. Think about the obstacles you overcame—the days you almost gave up, the moments you questioned your worth, and the nights you prayed for clarity. Let those memories anchor you, not distract you.

Here's the key: don't confuse rest with retreat. Celebration should replenish your energy, not cause you to abandon the mission. In fact, the aftermath of success is one of the most vulnerable spaces to be in —because once you taste accomplishment, the temptation to get comfortable is real. But purpose doesn't stop just because you hit one goal. If anything, new levels come with new assignments.

Another pitfall of unchecked celebration is the illusion of completion. Just because you accomplished one thing doesn't mean your work is done. Purpose evolves. Growth stretches. And your capacity is constantly expanding. If you stay too long in celebration mode, you risk letting a moment define you instead of letting it develop you.

You also have to be mindful of your posture after the win. Are you still teachable? Are you still hungry? Are you still sensitive to the people assigned to your voice, your gifts, or your calling? If not, you may have celebrated too long in isolation and forgotten your why.

Your celebration must be rooted in purpose, not ego. Because if it becomes about proving a point rather than making an impact, you'll lose sight of the bigger picture. Your success isn't just about what you gained—it's also about what you're meant to give back.

The truth is, celebration is a form of stewardship. It's your opportunity to give glory to God, acknowledge your growth, honor those who helped you, and remind yourself that this is bigger than you. But don't stay at the party so long that you miss your next assignment. Celebrate with joy—but keep your shoes on. There's still more ground to cover.

MAINTAINING THE BALANCE: CELEBRATE, THEN REFOCUS

Growing up as a pastor's kid, I often felt scrutinized—eyes always watching, expectations always looking. The unspoken pressure to be perfect, to perform, to represent well—it all created a quiet narrative in my mind that nothing I did was ever enough. Even when I achieved something significant, the celebration was short-lived, if it happened at all. The question that always followed was, "What's next?"

That pattern made it hard for me to fully embrace joy. I minimized my wins and sped past milestones because I had internalized the idea that accomplishment without continued performance wasn't worth acknowledging. But over time, I've learned something transformative: celebrating your wins is not only healthy—it's holy. It's an act of honoring the process, recognizing your growth, and affirming that what you've done matters.

Celebration doesn't make you complacent. It makes you present. It anchors you in truth—the truth that you are worthy of pausing, breathing, and smiling at how far you've come.

Still, maintaining the balance between celebration and momentum is a discipline. It's easy to get stuck in either extreme—celebrating so long that you lose focus, or skipping celebration altogether and staying in constant grind mode. True growth lies in the middle.

Here's what that balance looks like: take time to honor your effort. If no one else throws a party for you, throw your own. Take yourself out. Reflect on the internal battles you've conquered and the quiet progress no one saw but God. Journal the lesson. Speak gratitude aloud. And then—*refocus*.

Don't confuse resting in the moment with retiring from the mission. The purpose doesn't stop because you crossed one finish line. If anything, it expands. Celebration should fill your tank, not signal the end of the race.

Ask yourself: "What did this win teach me?", "Who do I need to thank or uplift?", and "What new doors does this open for me to serve others?" When celebration includes reflection and vision, it becomes a launching pad—not a landing place.

Legacy builders know how to pause with purpose. They don't rush past the win, but they also don't camp out in it forever. They celebrate and recalibrate.

So yes—stand on the podium. Take the victory lap. Let the confetti fall. But once it settles, lace up again with more courage, more clarity, and more capacity than before.

Because your journey doesn't end with applause—it evolves with purpose. And the best part? There's still more in you. You're just getting started.

THE DANGERS OF COMFORT ZONES

Comfort zones are silent killers of purpose. They disguise themselves as peace, but often it's just passivity. You feel "settled," but deep down, you know you've stopped stretching. The truth is, comfort is often the counterfeit of calling. It makes you think you've arrived when, really, you've only paused.

There's a false sense of security that comes from knowing your routine, your strengths, your titles. But titles can become traps. The moment you begin to live off yesterday's accomplishments, you start drifting from the momentum that once made you effective. The energy that once pushed you toward purpose becomes dulled by predictability. You're no longer growing—you're just existing in a cycle of "good enough."

And here's the thing about stagnation: it doesn't announce itself loudly. It settles in slowly. First, you delay one task. Then you defer one decision. Then suddenly, weeks have passed and you're still rehearsing the same goals without any real movement. That's not rest —it's retreat in disguise.

To break free, you have to interrupt your own rhythm. Disrupt what's become easy. Say yes to what challenges you. Chase after what requires new capacity, deeper faith, and higher vision. Ask yourself questions that force you to stretch.

For example:

- What am I avoiding that I know would grow me?
- Who am I becoming if I stay here?
- What part of my calling is dying in the name of comfort?

Comfort zones don't just affect you, they rob the world of your voice, your ideas, and your God-given impact. Someone is waiting on the version of you that only emerges when you leave the shallow end and swim in deeper waters. Every time you shrink back, you forfeit that encounter. Every time you choose the easy path, someone else's breakthrough is delayed.

That's why growth requires friction. You weren't designed to be static. You're called to evolve, stretch, and rise. And sometimes, the most spiritual thing you can do is challenge your comfort and say, "This is no longer enough for who I'm becoming."

Refuse to settle for the version of you that is accepted but unfulfilled, applauded but unstretched, familiar but not free. Let every layer of comfort that no longer serves you be a signal—it's time to move. You have more to become.

MAINTAINING MOMENTUM

Momentum doesn't just happen, it's a mindset. It's what you choose after the celebration ends. True momentum means understanding that success is not a finish line—it's a foundation. What you do after the applause matters just as much as what you did to earn it.

Many people slow down after hitting a milestone because they confuse arrival with assignment. But milestones are meant to be markers, not memorials. If you're not careful, your last win can become your last movement. And that's not how legacy is built. Legacy lives in motion.

One of the greatest ways to keep moving forward is to make your success transferable. That means extracting the lessons from your journey and creating pathways for others to walk through. Don't just share the highlight reel—share the behind-the-scenes. Let people see the mistakes, the pivots, the questions you had to wrestle with. That's where real mentorship begins.

And mentorship isn't always formal. Sometimes it's a post you write, a workshop you teach, or simply showing up consistently as someone others can watch. It's living out your growth in such a way that it becomes contagious. When people see you walking in purpose, they begin to believe they can, too.

Sustained momentum also requires that you stay curious. Ask new questions. Set new benchmarks. Surround yourself with people who aren't impressed by what you've done, but inspired by what you could do next. Let those people stretch you. Let their hunger remind you to stay full—not of ego, but of purpose.

Don't just ride the wave of your last breakthrough—build new ones. Innovate. Iterate. Expand. Every lesson you've learned can be repurposed into a tool for someone else's journey. Whether it's in business, ministry, education, or life, you have the power to multiply your impact when you share the wisdom behind your wins.

And as you pour into others, you'll find that your fire doesn't burn out—it grows. Because when purpose fuels progress, the momentum never ends.

CELEBRATE YOUR WINS, THEN PUSH FORWARD

True success is not just measured by what you accomplish—but by how you respond once you do.

It's easy to let momentum slip through your fingers the moment applause fades. The temptation to slow down, to bask in the validation, can quietly lead to stagnation if not met with intentionality. That's why after every win—whether personal, spiritual, or professional—you must immediately ask yourself, "What's next?" Not out of pressure, but out of purpose.

Every win is a doorway, not a destination. Each success gives you a vantage point you didn't have before. From that higher place, you can see further, dream bigger, and serve deeper. But only if you keep moving. That's the paradox of purpose—it rewards rest but requires readiness.

The most impactful leaders understand this. They know how to celebrate the moment while still being anchored in the mission. Like seasoned runners crossing one finish line only to prepare for the next race, they train their minds to expect more, not out of greed, but out of grace. Because they recognize the gift of achievement is never just for them—it's for those coming after.

Think of it like climbing a mountain. Reaching the summit is a victory. But the view from the top often reveals other peaks you couldn't see before. The climb sharpened your skills, tested your endurance, and built your resilience. But it also prepared you for greater ascents. So take in the view—but don't unpack your bags.

And while you're on the journey, don't forget the map you just created. Every time you break through a barrier, you hold the blueprint for someone else's breakthrough. That's what made Harriet Tubman a legend. It wasn't just that she found freedom—it was that she returned to lead others to it. Her victory wasn't validated until it was multiplied.

Likewise, your success gains meaning when it moves beyond you. When your testimony becomes someone else's turning point. When your victory lap becomes someone else's starting line.

So, toast the win. Rest when needed. But don't take your shoes off yet. There's still work to do, still people to reach, still dreams to unlock. Let each win awaken your hunger—not just for more, but for more impact.

You didn't come this far to stop here.

CHAPTER 8 APPLICATION

Learning to celebrate without becoming complacent is a spiritual discipline. Victory is a gift, but it's not the end of your story. In this chapter, you learned that the goal isn't just to win—it's to keep walking in purpose after the win. Let's break that down practically.

Step 1: Reflect on Your Latest Victory

Think of a recent win—big or small. It could be something spiritual, professional, relational, or personal.

- What did you accomplish?
- How did you celebrate?
- Did the celebration cause you to pause your momentum or reignite it?

Write down your reflections:

_____

_____

_____

Recent Victory:

_____

_____

_____

How I Celebrated:

_____

_____

_____

Did I lose focus or gain clarity afterward?

_____

_____

_____

Step 2: Check for Complacency

Even good things can become distractions when we get too comfortable.

List 2–3 areas of your life where comfort may be creeping in.

Comfort Zones to Examine:

1. _____
2. _____
3. _____

Now, write a short statement about to each identifying why you're choosing not to settle there.

_____

_____

_____

_____

_____

_____

_____

_____

_____

_____

_____

_____

Step 3: Revive the Vision

Victories are not endings; they are checkpoints. Look at the bigger vision God gave you. What comes next?

What dream or assignment has been on pause since the last win?

_____

_____

_____

_____

_____

_____

What does "obedience after the win" look like in your life right now?

_____

_____

_____

_____

_____

_____

Step 4: Create a Post-Victory Action Plan

Use the space below to map out what comes after your celebration. Write down your _victory_, _next step_, and _obedience action_, as it pertains to each area listed below.

Spiritual

_____

_____

_____

_____

Personal

_____
_____
_____
_____
_____

Purpose

_____
_____
_____
_____
_____

Relationships

_____
_____
_____
_____
_____

Step 5: Embrace the Weight in the Wait

Before every next level, there's a stretch. Just like a seed planted in the ground needs good soil, your next season requires preparation.

Reflection:

- Have I truly planted my vision in good soil (a surrendered heart)?
- What spiritual nourishment am I providing daily?
- Am I rushing the harvest?

Write down your response:

_____
_____
_____
_____
_____
_____
_____
_____
_____
_____
_____
_____

Step 6: Write a Declaration

Write a personal declaration that reminds you to celebrate, but not settle.

Example: *"I will celebrate this victory with gratitude, but I won't stop here. I am still called, still growing, and still moving. God is not finished with me yet."*

Now write your own:

_____
_____
_____
_____
_____
_____
_____
_____
_____
_____

Key Takeaways

If you take nothing else from this chapter, let it be this:

1. *Celebrations are sacred,* but so is what comes next.

2. *Comfort zones can camouflage themselves as "peace."* Be alert.

3. *Every victory plants seeds for the next season;* make sure they're in good soil.

4. *God is still working* in you, through you, and beyond you.

* * *

You've had your victory lap. Now it's time to get back in the race. *Let's go.*

DON'T TAKE YOUR SHOES OFF YET

W e live in a culture that often equates comfort with success. The moment we hit a milestone or check off a goal, we're tempted to rest, assuming the work is done. But what if that moment isn't the finish line, but merely a checkpoint?

Comfort can be deceptive—it tells you you've arrived when you've only just begun. It whispers, "Relax," when your next assignment is waiting. That's why you can't take your shoes off just yet. There's still ground to cover, still people waiting on the other side of your obedience, and still purpose left unfulfilled.

When you're deeply connected to your purpose, you begin to recognize that the celebration of success is not a call to retire—it's a signal to reinforce. Every level of achievement is an invitation to reevaluate: Who needs what I've learned? How can I multiply this impact? What doors did this open—and who am I supposed to usher through?

Many people mistake accomplishment for arrival. But the truth is, arrival without assignment becomes idleness. That's why purpose is so important. It keeps you grounded when praise starts to inflate you. It reminds you that the applause isn't the goal—it's the echo of impact.

Even in seasons when everything looks great externally—good

marriage, thriving business, financial freedom—there can be an unshakable restlessness. That's not a void to fear. That's often God's whisper reminding you, "There's more." Not necessarily more stuff—but more significance.

And purpose is never passive. It pulls you out of bed when you're tired. It challenges you to grow when you'd rather stay comfortable. It refuses to let you settle. Why? Because purpose isn't about you—it's about legacy. It's about being faithful with the gifts you've been given so that someone else can find freedom through your yes.

In nearly every faith tradition, calling and purpose are deeply inter-twined with service. Whether it's through acts of compassion, sharing knowledge, lifting others, or living with integrity—your purpose is validated through its impact on people. So if you've been wondering why you still feel a pull even after success—it's likely because someone needs what you've been given.

Don't be fooled by polished photos and picture-perfect stories. The real question isn't whether your life looks full—it's whether it feels fulfilled. Fulfillment lives at the intersection of calling and contribution.

So keep going. Don't take your shoes off. There are still paths to carve, people to uplift, and promises waiting on the other side of your persistence. *The work isn't finished—because you're not finished.*

WHEN PURPOSE IS STILL CALLING

If you're restless, it's not by accident—it's an alert from your spirit that you've only scratched the surface. There's something sacred about that inner stirring. It's not dissatisfaction in a negative sense; it's divine discontent nudging you toward your next level. If you're sensing there's more, you're right—and that awareness is proof that your purpose still has room to stretch.

Purpose doesn't just fill time; it fills lives. It wakes up your passion, reorders your priorities, and causes you to ask bigger ques-tions. You'll know you're walking in your purpose when what you're doing no longer feels like a performance but a release. There's ease in it—not because it's always simple, but because it feels aligned.

Let's be clear: being good at something doesn't mean it's your calling. Many of us have mastered skills out of necessity or survival—jobs we're proficient in, but not passionate about. Purpose, however, has a unique fingerprint. It doesn't just bless your life—it multiplies into the lives of others. It doesn't drain you, it draws more out of you.

The reason you can't settle is because what you've done so far isn't the end of your assignment—it's the entry point. You're not exhausted because you're finished; you're weary because you've been working from duty, not destiny. But when you begin to walk in purpose, there's an undeniable sense of fulfillment—even when you're tired.

The meal metaphor still holds: don't serve something half-baked. When God gives you a vision, He also expects stewardship. Presentation matters. Timing matters. Preparation matters. And just like with a gourmet dish, even one uncooked element compromises the entire experience. Your life is no different. Don't rush to the table of impact before you've spent time in the kitchen of refinement.

And don't withhold the meal. What God placed in you wasn't meant to be hoarded or hidden. It was meant to feed nations—sometimes literally, sometimes emotionally, spiritually, or intellectually. When you hold back your gift, you deny others access to healing, clarity, and breakthrough that may only come through your voice, your story, your obedience.

Ask yourself: What have I been doing well that isn't actually what I was born to do? What fills others but empties me? What do I do naturally, joyfully, and with a sense of flow that feels connected to something higher?

Your answers will guide you toward the more you've been sensing. But don't just sense it—pursue it. The world is starving for what you've been preparing. You just can't take your shoes off yet.

CULTIVATING CONTINUOUS GROWTH

True growth doesn't happen in bursts—it's a lifestyle choice. It's the daily decision to rise above comfort, stretch beyond what's familiar, and say "yes" to the version of you that's still becoming. Growth doesn't stop once you've reached a major milestone. In fact, real growth begins after the first mountain is climbed, when you realize there are still entire ranges to scale.

One of the most underrated truths about continuous growth is this: who you walk with determines where you end up. You can be the most talented, passionate, or visionary person in the room, but if you're always the smartest one in your circle, you've outgrown your environment. You need voices that call you higher, not ones that coddle your comfort. Growth demands proximity to greatness.

But don't confuse noise with nourishment. Not everyone who speaks into your life will speak life into you. Cultivating growth means surrounding yourself with those who model where you're headed—people whose values, discipline, and excellence challenge your own. These aren't just mentors or role models—they're mirrors, revealing where you are and who you're capable of becoming.

Build a team or find partners who refuse to let you grow complacent. True friends or mentors will remind you of your vision and push you to keep striving. They'll know when you're simply tired and when you're veering into self-sabotage. Keep people around you who not only believe in your purpose but hold you accountable to it. You were never meant to grow in isolation. Your next level is often locked inside a conversation, a partnership, or a challenge that only the right people can deliver.

Create a vision board. Write the vision plainly. Put it where you can see it. Then review it regularly. Set new goals every few months—goals that scare you a little and stretch you a lot. If you reached $100K, aim for $250K. If you've impacted 10 people, strategize how to reach 100. Growth doesn't come from maintaining what was; it comes from pursuing what could be.

And here's the truth: every new level of success requires a new level of discipline and a greater depth of humility. What got you here won't get you there. So keep adjusting. Successful individuals don't stay the same—they pivot, refine, and recalibrate. They remain teachable and flexible, knowing that agility is the key to long-term impact.

To maintain momentum, your boundaries must mature along with your vision. The "yes" you gave at the beginning of your journey may no longer serve you. New levels require new limits. You don't have to apologize for evolving. As you ascend, not everyone can go with you—and that's okay. Growth doesn't isolate you, but it does refine your relationships.

Discipline isn't just about grinding harder; it's about being deeply intentional. It's the art of making strategic decisions that align with your long-term vision, not your short-term emotions. Consistency, then, becomes the vehicle for transformation. Even when progress feels slow, each step forward compounds, shaping who you become.

And never forget: continuous growth isn't only about you. When you grow, you stretch what's possible for others. You become evidence that elevation is attainable. You become a roadmap. A lighthouse. A standard.

Here's a powerful exercise to remind you what's at stake:

Close your eyes and visualize a number between one and a million. Don't overthink it—just let the number rise in your spirit. Whatever number comes to mind, write it at the very beginning and the very end of this book. One at the front. One at the back.

Why? Because that number represents the lives connected to your obedience—the people whose mental, spiritual, or emotional breakthrough might be delayed because your purpose is still sitting dormant.

So if you ever find yourself returning to this book—whether it's months or years from now—you'll see that number before you start and again as you close. It's a gentle reminder. A wake-up call. A quiet push.

That number is not arbitrary. It symbolizes how many people are potentially dying every day you choose to stay stagnant. Not just physically—but mentally, spiritually, emotionally—because your vision was never released. That many people are staying stuck because the healing, wisdom, or inspiration you were called to share is still trapped inside of you.

This exercise isn't to guilt you, but to stir something deeper in you. It's a reminder that your delay isn't neutral. Purpose always has a ripple effect.

So the next time you're tempted to procrastinate...

The next time comfort feels easier than consistency...

The next time you think, "I've done enough"...

Go back to that number.

And get back to work.

Your greatest motivation should always come from knowing the impact of your purpose on others. People are gateways to your next level—your success and purpose are inherently connected to serving and uplifting others. If your actions aren't serving someone else, you're not fully living your purpose. Your journey is incomplete until it positively affects others. Love for people is inseparable from love for God. Staying mindful of the broader impact of your purpose will continuously renew your motivation.

CHAPTER 9 APPLICATION

There's a difference between finishing something and fulfilling your assignment. Sometimes, success will tempt you to settle, but legacy demands that you go further. This chapter challenges you to reflect on what's left in your hands—even when others think the work is done.

Let's walk through it step by step.

Step 1: Check for Comfort Zones

Where in your life have you mentally "taken your shoes off" even though the assignment isn't finished?

Write down 3–5 areas where you may have paused your purpose:

1. _____
2. _____
3. _____
4. _____
5. _____

What made you stop or slow down? Check all that apply:

☐ Burnout
☐ Distraction
☐ Comfort
☐ Fear
☐ Feeling Unqualified
☐ Comparison

Now reflect: What was the last thing God told you to do in that area?

_____
_____
_____

Step 2: Discern the Difference Between Rest and Retreat

Rest is biblical. Retreating from purpose is not. Think of a time you rested in a healthy way. Now think of a time you quit too soon.

Healthy Rest Example:

_____

_____

_____

_____

_____

_____

_____

Premature Retreat Example:

_____

_____

_____

_____

_____

_____

_____

What's one thing you can do this week to rest without quitting?

_____

_____

_____

_____

_____

_____

_____

Step 3: Name What's Still in You

You've come far, but you're not done yet. Your gifts still matter. List 3–5 gifts, skills, or passions God has given you that you haven't fully used yet:

1. _____
2. _____
3. _____
4. _____
5. _____

Who still needs what's inside of you? List at least 2 people or groups:

1. _____
2. _____

What will it cost them if you quit too early?

_____
_____
_____
_____
_____
_____

Step 4: Take One Bold Next Step

Write one small but significant action step you can take this week to move forward in your assignment—even if it's uncomfortable:

_____
_____
_____
_____

Now write out a declaration you can speak over yourself to stay encouraged:

Example: I will not stop until I've poured out everything God placed inside of me. My journey is not over.

Write yours here:

_____

_____

_____

_____

Step 5: Seed Check – Are You Planted in Good Soil?

Growth doesn't happen just because you're active. It happens because you're planted.

Use this section to reflect on your soil—your heart, your mindset, and your environment.

- Is your current soil nourishing your growth or choking it?
- Are you surrounded by people and places that align with God's plan for you?

Write your reflection:

_____

_____

_____

_____

_____

_____

_____

What changes do you need to make to be planted in good ground?

_____

_____

_____

_____

Key Takeaways

If you take nothing else from this chapter, let it be this:

1. *Your journey isn't over* just because you've achieved something.

2. *Let rest refresh you*, but don't confuse it with retreat.

3. *You're still carrying* something the world needs.

4. *Plant yourself in good soil* and stay committed to the process.

5. *The finish line is not success*—it's fulfillment.

* * *

You're not done yet. *Lace up. Show up. Pour out.* There's more in you. And there's more ahead.

OBEDIENCE IN MOTION

You've trekked through every chapter, wrestled with identity, purpose, boundaries, momentum, and the weight of waiting. Now you're standing at the threshold between learning and living. Before you close this book, lace your shoes tighter—because the road ahead is where the real transformation happens.

This moment marks a shift—from reflection to action, from breakthrough to becoming. Everything you've read has been preparation, not finality. The healing you've begun, the truth you've uncovered, and the clarity you've gained are only the starting blocks of the next lap in your journey.

This metaphor—*don't take your shoes off yet*—symbolizes the commitment to keep going even when the path is long, the terrain is rough, and your soul craves comfort. It means you haven't arrived just because you've survived. You haven't completed the assignment just because you've accomplished something. There is still more inside you. More to give. More to build. More to become.

Taking your shoes off prematurely means letting up before the work is truly done. It's the temptation to settle in a space God never told you to stop. It's when you start living off of yesterday's momentum, satisfied with the illusion of arrival while your true calling waits patiently for your obedience.

Shoes, in this context, represent readiness, movement, and mission. They are the spiritual and emotional armor that remind you to keep walking, even when it hurts. The discomfort you feel—blisters of the soul, sore feet from carrying heavy burdens, the ache of delayed promises—is not a reason to stop. It is proof that you're stretching, pressing, and growing. It's evidence that you're in motion.

Imagine a journey where every step matters. You've walked miles and miles in your purpose, and now your feet are throbbing. You're tired. You're successful by many standards. But deep down, you know something's still unfinished. That's the moment where most people check out. They assume it's time to coast. But this moment? This is the most critical stretch of your race.

This is where champions are made—not because they're the fastest or the strongest—but because they kept going when everyone else took their shoes off.

There will be moments where rest is necessary. God honors rest, and He gives it intentionally. But rest is different from retirement. Don't confuse the two. Rest replenishes. Completion releases. And unless you've been released by the One who gave you the assignment, your shoes need to stay on.

The road ahead might not be smooth. But it's intentional. Keep walking. Keep pressing. Keep your shoes on—because the next step could be the one that breaks the chains off someone else's life.

You're not just walking for you. You're walking for those who will come after you. So tighten the laces, adjust your pace if you must, but never stop moving forward. Your journey is not over.

Not yet.

ACKNOWLEDGMENTS

To everyone who walked with me, carried me, challenged me, and believed in this work — thank you. I cannot name you all, but please know that every word here was made possible by your presence in my life.

To my people — my family by blood and by design, my friends who became anchors, the prophets who spoke truth when I forgot it, and those who held me with love and without judgment — your support has been the quiet strength beneath every step I've taken. You listened, prayed, pushed, laughed, cried, and stayed. Whether through a single conversation or a consistent presence, you helped me keep going when it would have been easier to stop.

To those who shaped this work with care and intention — thank you. Your insight, time, honest feedback, and patience helped turn fragments into something whole. You honored the heart of the work while helping it breathe clearer, speak louder, and stand stronger.

And to the version of me who kept showing up — I see you. I'm proud of your resilience, your vulnerability, and your trust in the process. This is a testament to your persistence and your courage to keep writing, even when it felt like no one was listening.

This is not just mine — it's ours. A reflection of all the voices, hearts, and hands that touched it along the way. Thank you for being part of the journey.

ABOUT THE AUTHOR

Jonathan Allen, Jr. is not afraid to admit he's still figuring life out. Like many, he's wrestled with procrastination, fear, and self-doubt—but also discovered the power of faith, resilience, and showing up anyway.

As a life coach, speaker, and now author, Jonathan uses his own journey as proof that you don't have to have it all together to take the next step. His message is simple: *keep going, because your purpose is still waiting for you.*